Who Am I
Really?

Who Am I Really?

Shari Arison
Nurit Eldar

YBK Publishers NEW YORK

Who Am I Really?

YBK Publishers, Inc.
39 Crosby Street
New York, NY 10013
www.ybkpublishers.com

ISBN: 978-1-936411-77-1

Library of Congress Cataloging-in-Publication Data
[LC record applied for]

Manufactured in the United States of America for distribution in
North and South America or in the United Kingdom or Australia
when distributed elsewhere.

For more information, visit
www.ybkpublishers.com

Preface

by Shari Arison

I am Shari Arison, daughter of the late Ted Arison and the late Mina Arison Sapir. I am the mother of four children, the grandmother of six grandchildren, and I am involved in a wide range of endeavors.

I have been undergoing a spiritual process for forty years; a process that, as I see it, will never end. In this book I invite you into this process, but before we begin the journey, I would like to briefly introduce you to the activities in which I am involved.

For many years, I have been deeply engaged in business and philanthropy. I was a member of the boards of directors of both public and private companies and I have managed businesses and organizations that were, and still are, a world of their own. In partnership with several collaborators, I established a chain of roadside restaurants and rest areas within the Mövenpick franchise, including one in Tel Aviv. I loved those restaurants, but, regrettably, among other reasons, I had to close them due to the security situation in Israel at the time.

Through the business arm of the Arison Group, Arison Investments, I founded Miya—a global water-efficiency company, the purpose of which was to realize the vision of bringing an abundance of pure water to the world. I was also the owner of several other businesses operating in the fields of banking, infrastructure, real estate, water, renewable energy, and the salt industry.

I have always led businesses that bring added value to people; to their society, to the environment, and to the economy.

For many years, I strived to change the "systems" as a whole. We were successful in many of these endeavors, and less so in other aspects, but, after realizing that I was no longer creating the positive change I continued to want to make, I decided to sell my companies and transition into a model of influence that did not require ownership.

Today, through Arison Investments, I invest in a wide range of global industries that bring added value to humanity. In this way, I am able to continue to create impact from a harmonious, creative, and very enjoyable place, by focusing on initiatives that bring immense added value to our planet and to humanity at large.

Over the course of many years, I developed "The Doing Good Model" (dgm.life)—a practical, day-to-day tool for integrating values at the core of businesses, nonprofits, communities, and among individuals. The model incorporates thirteen universal values to apply to any endeavor as a moral compass. This model is taught at George Mason University in the U.S.A. The organization, The Doing Good Model, guides value implementation in businesses and organizations in Israel and worldwide.

In my late father's name, I founded The Ted Arison Family Foundation in the U.S.A. in the 1980s and in Israel in the 1990s. It is a privately held family fund that makes contributions in a wide range of fields.

I have led many projects in health, education, research, and the arts—being always personally involved in all of the detail, from start to end. Through The Ted Arison Family Foundation, I have founded vision ventures that continue independently without my daily involvement such as Matan (matanisrael.org) that I had led for many years that has established a culture of giving among many members of the Israeli business community.

Over the years, I have founded and led many similar ventures:

Essence of Life, which operates to raise awareness and provide tools for inner peace. This organization runs an Internet radio station, a website, and a visitor's center called Mahuti in Tel Aviv (mahuti.co.il).

Goodnet (goodnet.org), a social web platform in English, which inspires doing good by connecting people and organizations worldwide that do good.

Ruach Tova (Hebrew for Good Spirit— ruachtova.org. il), is an organization adopted by The Ted Arison Family Foundation to encourage the spirit of volunteering in Israel by matching volunteers with organizations that seek volunteers. As a part of this framework, I initiated and continue to lead Good Deeds Day, a global day that is a peak event celebrating the year-round activities of doing good that is celebrated by millions of people in more than 108 countries across the globe.

I am extremely thrilled that all of my business and philanthropic activities are operated together with my children, along with a management team and employees, who, like me, are committed to this work and have a sense of mission.

Forbes Magazine has repeatedly ranked me as one of the most influential women in the world, placing me second in its world's greenest billionaires list for my environmental contributions in Israel and worldwide, which also translates into business dealings.

I have been named Honorary Fellow of the Decade by the Interdisciplinary Center Herzliya (IDC), where I served on its board of directors, and I have received the America-Israel Friendship League (AIFL) award for my contribution to promoting the economies of Israel and America. I hold an Honorary Doctorate of Humane Letters from George Mason University, in appreciation for "advancing and implementing values-based business and philanthropy," and I have been honored with the Medal of Light (Itur Ha`or) from the Knesset (Israeli Parliament) for The Ted Arison Family Foundation's proactivity toward Holocaust survivors and for my activities within Israeli society that benefit the State of Israel.

I have published eight books, which became instant bestsellers in Israel and worldwide and have been translated into numerous languages. In my books, I write from the heart and share my journey to inspire awareness and positive change. My books are written from different angles in diverse fields—spirituality, business, giving, art, and children's books: Birth, When the Material and the Spiritual Come Together; Activate Your Goodness; Material for Thought; The Doing Good Model; A Day of Good Deeds; and Or's Journey.

I adore animals, and I love to paint and create. I voice myself on social media and I host radio shows, all for the sake of fulfilling my goal and greatest passion—helping people to connect with their own selves, their very essence and soul, by finding that divine spark within themselves.

So far I have described myself to you by using definitions, but, in this book, you will get an inner glimpse into the inside of me, into who I really am. My activities and degrees do not reflect how I feel inside: powerful or weak; happy or sad. Does the outer world reflect my inner world, and vice versa? Am I vital and calm? Do I feel that my soul's aspiration and calling are being realized? Truly, all the activities and degrees have nothing to do with what lives inside me (or what it is that lives within all of us).

I met Nurit, my partner-author in this book, when a director, serving on the board of a company that I owned, gifted me her book, Letters from Heaven, saying that only after he read her book, did he finally come to understand what I have been talking about for so many years.

This intrigued me. I read Nurit's book in just two days, and for someone whose mother tongue is not Hebrew, who normally reads books in English, this was no trivial matter. I decided that I had to get to know the woman who wrote this book, expressing so well, and in such straight-forward, simple language, some of the things that I have been talking about for years.

And, so it was. With the universe sending me so many messages stating that I must meet her, I initiated a meeting. From our first minutes together I felt an immediate and deep connection—like electricity running between us. We both knew a book would come out of this, although we only first spoke about it at a much later time.

That is how we started our journey together—a journey that is a connection between two women who came together with different viewpoints, backgrounds, and spiritual perspectives—yet resulted in a deep and profound friendship.

Work on the book began in 2018. It was a process of continuing evolution, during which we asked ourselves several times whether we should continue or stop. Whether this suited us or not? Was it important to us that a book come out of our meetings, or was it, perhaps, the meetings themselves that were the important construct? We continued to walk this path together. Each time we met it seemed as if it is had been ages since the last time we had seen each other. Everything held new meaning and fresh insight as we experienced a major transition between each meeting and the next.

Then, in the beginning of 2020, I fell ill and almost left my body. For almost two weeks I was so ill I communicated with no one. I almost did not even open my eyes. I could eat nothing.

For four days during this time, while my physical body was bedridden, my soul was in a kind of negotiation about staying here.

I wanted to stay for my children. I saw them before my eyes all of the time—saying to myself that I am ready to die, but not yet—not yet, because I want to be with them.

I was told that when the time comes to die, it will be time.

I agreed and understood.

I was shown space, the Earth, and I was told that evolution happens on its own. I did not understand what they wanted to tell me.

When I left my sickbed and returned to the ground, to the "here and now," still very weak, I was depressed.

What does this mean? Does it mean that all that interests me are my children?

They have always been the most important thing in my life. But the mission—is it the mission that is so important to me? This never crossed my mind.

And, if evolution happens on its own, what does that say about my mission?

After eleven days, I returned to work slowly, exhausted and sad. What do I do now? What does this mean regarding all of my activities? All my endeavors?

I carried on and continued my work, but I did not really understand why.

And then Coronavirus hit.

"Evolution happens on its own." This message was suddenly very accurate. I understood what my mission was now.

We have all returned to our homes. Our health and our family has taken the front of the stage. I now look at all that I have built and done until this day in a new and different light.

I see that my mission is to be—to bring light, hope, and faith. Simply, to love.

I wish you pleasant reading, and hope that each and every one of you will get from this book something that will help you on your inner journey of personal development and growth.

I wish for you that you will get to know who you are, really.

With love,
Shari Arison

Preface

by Nurit Eldar

The most incredible journey of my life; a journey that shook me, thrilled me, and, most importantly, helped me to get back to my true self, began with a single statement I heard in the year 2000, when I was an arts therapy graduate student at Lesley University in Cambridge, Massachusetts.

"Nurit, you draw symbols taken from the world of Native Americans. Do you have a connection to Native American culture?"

This occurred during a lesson at the university, at a workshop concerning stream of consciousness drawing. For the life of me, I could not understand what the teacher meant, nor why she would ask me this question. I had never had a specific interest in Native Americans, nor was I particularly interested in their culture and civilization. How on earth, then, was I be able to draw Native American motifs? I determined that this entire incident was attributable to pure chance.

Much of the work we did in my university studies involved intuitive creativity through drawing, painting, and sculpt-

ing. We attempted to express emotions through the arts; not through tangible meanings. There was no value placed on beauty or aesthetics, only on free expression. The ability to create something on a full or an empty page or canvas— without consciously thinking—gave me much pleasure. It was much more than that, though. I felt that something inside of me had opened. It was an intense and deeply emotional and thrilling process.

Then the dreams began. I began spending my sleeping nights flying. I was soaring in the sky, taking flight over vast distances. This was a new experience; different from anything I had ever experienced, and thrilling though it was, it held some terrifying aspects. I could not understand what was happening. Many thoughts raced through my mind. I turned to my teacher to ask for her help. She sought to calm me by explaining that this was a known phenomenon, and that I was blessed.

But her words did little to comfort me. On the contrary, they pushed me even deeper into panic. I felt strange. Finally, my fear overcame these dreams.

I experienced a short, quiet break from those thoughts, but then, gradually, I began to recognize that I now knew things about the people around me. I could look at someone's drawings and simply know things about that person far beyond what had been drawn by them. Eventually, I decided that I had some sort of gift—that I was an "Art Therapy Reader."

This comforted me, enabling me to go on with my life as usual as I tried to suppress these thoughts into a far corner of my mind where they would not disturb the daily routine of the rational, practical world in which I lived. (I was at the time a major in the air force, after all; a serious-minded, responsible officer.)

I could not have known, nor even guessed, that I was at just the beginning of a magical journey that would completely change my life.

I grew up in a very rational-minded home. Logic and intelligence were the cornerstones from which we observed life. I was drawn to the world of the exact sciences. In high school, I majored in mathematics and physics. I served in the air force as a meteorology officer, going on to study architecture at the Israel Institute of Technology. It took two-and-a-half years for me to realize that the profession of architecture did not sufficiently interest me. Something was missing. I considered completely changing direction, but, as I had already completed almost three years of the five-year course of study, I decided to finish my degree before making any change.

From the time of that decision, until about four years after my graduation, I was on a self-seeking quest that provided no significant results. While I successfully fitted into the business world, I did not feel it was where I genuinely belonged.

In 1992, by coincidence (I do not, of course, believe this was a coincidence, but, instead, divine guidance), I received an offer to return to military service as a standing army architecture officer in the air force's construction and development department. During my service, I began to understand that I was a "people person." It had taken some time to realize that an inner voice was urging me to make a change.

In 2000, I began studying for a master's degree in art therapy at Lesley University. It was at Lesley that "it" opened for me. (I purposely use the word "it" because I had no way of defining what was happening to me.)

It took until 2005, again seemingly by coincidence, to realize that I had "channeling" abilities.

I made it to be a big secret. I felt uncomfortable with it.

My world view was rational and practical. Nearly all

of my friends were engineers. My sister was a lawyer. My brother was a senior computer programmer. And what was I? What was this "thing" I now possessed? On the one hand, I did not want it. On the other, I was very much drawn to it. There was some inexplicable magic involved.

This was the beginning of my journey into the knowledge and wisdom beyond. It is a journey that I have been on for twenty years. It continues to enrich me, to teach me, and to surprise me.

In the year 2005, I finished my army service and began to seek my way in life. I felt uncomfortable about practicing channeling. I was afraid that people would mock me; fail to understand me. Mainly, though, I was afraid I might disappoint myself— that I might feel that it was nothing but nonsense—that I had allowed myself to get there without good reason.

I could not let go of the world of channeling because it held within it an intensity and a clarity I had never known before. However, I kept it a secret. Only a few people knew of my abilities. My fear of acknowledging my abilities caused me much confusion and prevented me from finding my path. This was a period of self and professional seeking. I knew I wanted to bring something significant and meaningful to the world, but I did not know exactly what it was, and I was afraid.

The significant turning point occurred in 2013, when I went to console a friend in my networking group whose husband had passed away. At that time, my friend, Dana Nissan and I had shared only a casual acquaintance. I had not known her newly deceased husband, Ilan, at all.

This was precisely why it was so emotional and empowering when Ilan suddenly began channeling me as Dana and I sat at the table in her garden during the Shiva call.

The conversation took place in my head, but it felt the same as any conversation with another person might feel. During the following year, I began to communicate messages between Ilan and Dana. It was an amazing period during which I was made aware of a vast knowledge about the soul's journey and the world beyond.

Dana empowered and supported me along this path, helping me in my struggle against the tremendous fear I felt inside—the fear that I might simply be inventing all of this.

Dana would tell me, "Everything is so precise. You relate things you couldn't possibly have known. This is in line with everything I've been currently reading about the world beyond."

Dana gave me the courage to continue as Ilan provided me with knowledge that made logical sense. His explanations fitted with my own way of thinking, making it easier for me to remain attentive and accepting. Ilan took me (in my consciousness) as a companion on his journey there. I experienced unique things I have not experienced since.

At the end of that year, my first book, "Letters from Heaven," was written with Dana. In that book Ilan reveals the story of souls after they have left this world. When the book was published, I knew my life would be forever changed. From that moment, I knew I had finally found my place in life. I began work in channeling; passing knowledge and teaching.

It was at that time that I parted from Ilan as a spiritual guide, but not before he connected me to The Council of Six, who accompany me in channeling and provide guidance to this very day. During the early months, my connection was mainly with Beyon, the leading guide of The Council of Six. Beyon had lived in our world until a few years ago. His name, as were the names of the other guides in the Council of Six, was chosen by me. He explains that, in the beyond, there are no names.

They communicate "energetically" and identify each other according to the "energetic signature" of each individual. Channeling without a defined name was difficult for me. Therefore, with his agreement, I chose to name him Beyon, short for Beyond, because the energetic meaning he channeled to me was one of determination—of being mission-driven, and of possessing foresight. He has managed to drive me to do things I would not have believed myself capable of doing. In our terms, Beyon is undoubtedly a true leader. Even at the early points of our relationship, Beyon had already presented me with ideas that I found far-reaching.

Among the five other guides in the group are two souls with masculine qualities and three souls with feminine qualities. In the world beyond, there is not male or female form because there is no physical body. There are, though, energies that are more feminine or more masculine in nature. Mostly, I find myself addressing the guides of the Council of Six according to their sex, male or female, even though it isn't so.

When I first met the guides, I felt their essence and the distinct value each one brought, but when I asked them for their names, because one can't really be expected to converse with another being over time without even knowing their name, they replied that I could call them by any name I saw fit to choose. I realized that I could recognize each according to the subject of the messages they brought, and named them accordingly:

Couri — From the word courage, who mainly speaks about fear and the ways of coping with it.

Yoshi — From the Hebrew word for integrity, "Yoshra," who brings direct and practical observation through science.

Faith — Who speaks of the freedom to believe in what has been chosen.

Joy — Who brings a profound viewpoint at the way we conduct ourselves in life using humor and laughter.

Lovely — Who speaks of self-love and giving oneself credit and appreciation.

As a result of my work with the Council of Six, and the additional knowledge I acquired through them, I wrote the book, "The Journey to the Wisdom Beyond."

My third book was "Life in the Afterworld—According to Gideon Singer," written in collaboration with Gideon Singer's widow, Shira Moriel Singer. In the book, Gideon tells of his experiences during his last incarnation, and the insights he gained in the beyond.

The fourth book, "Late Conversations with Mother," looks at choosing one's family, parenthood, and the complex relationships that exist between parents and children. This book provides details from my childhood and life, exploring the gap between the concepts prevalent in the beyond and the human ones in this world.

I met Shari at the end of 2016. What started with hesitant, yet fascinating meetings, gradually developed into a close and mutually nurturing relationship. We began with personal conversations, but, soon enough, I felt that there had developed something far beyond. It is a relationship from which I have learned much, while also learning a great deal about myself. The subject of this book includes much of the story of my life; the search for the courage to listen inwardly and to be who I truly am.

I am accompanied on my journey by my husband, Hadi, and my four children, Eden, Ofir, Liron, and Shira. You give me the strength and the daily support to dare to follow the calling of my heart, and to believe and be who I am. My friends and students (who are far beyond students) also march beside me on this path; together we are creating a space for personal development and growth.

Nurit Eldar

The Journey of a Young Beautiful Child

Once upon a time there was a little girl, who was extremely unique. All the people in the land did not understand why this girl was so strange. When everyone was complaining, suffering and judging one another, this beautiful little child loved—loved everyone, everything.

"How strange that is," everyone thought. "How can you love nature and architecture? how can you love artists and logic? How can you love the popular and the unpopular?"

This was so strange in the land, that the girl herself started to think that she was strange.

"Something is wrong with her, she was too sensitive", she was told. "She cares too much", she was told. So, the years went by, and the little girl grew up believing she did not belong. She landed on the wrong planet. She was so judged, that she judged herself.

She grew farther and farther away from herself, her true self. her essence, trying to achieve approval from her surroundings. She worked hard to be understood, to be loved, but the world showed her otherwise. It showed her over and over that she was misunderstood, and as much love as she poured out to others, she always felt the love is not received and returned, quite the opposite. Over and over disappointed, pained, betrayed, her kind heart was used by others. Others saw her kindness as weakness and took advantage. And with that she went on to prove herself, to grow both within and without. She accomplished quite a lot – became rich and famous, built an empire and aspired others, but inside she was like a flower blowing in the wind, until she understood the world outside is an illusion. It is only there to reflect what needs to be dealt with in the inside.

And so, she began her journey from within, using others as tools for introspection Every thought every feeling a reflection.

The feelings were painful and often the fear grew, blaming again, being jealous again, angry again, and so forth. But she never forgot that it was only her responsibility to take charge of her own thoughts and feelings, and her actions.

Going within got easier and easier, making her way through the dark energy, accepting it and then cleansing it, making a way for a new energy to come inside her and around her. The reflections grew clearer and clearer, her will to be pure and peaceful was her focus. She knew she wanted to change the world she lived in, but in order to do that, she needed to change the world from within.

To change oneself is to change the entire world, as we are all connected, we are all one and everything is a reflection everything is an illusion, everything is

God. Each and every one of us is God, and to reach the God from within us is the ultimate journey. To live the God from within us is our purpose. This is evolution, this is paradise on earth, this is peace, this is love, and so be it.

Shari Arison

We Meet

I was sitting in my study when the phone rang. I did not recognize the caller's number.

I accepted the call and heard the pleasant voice of a young woman on the line. "I'm calling from Shari Arison's office. She has read your book, "Letters From Heaven," and would love to meet with you."

"What?" I asked, confused. "What do you mean?"

"Shari would like to meet you. She enjoyed your book."

Very intriguing, I thought, and, of course, I wanted to meet her!

Back then, all I knew about Shari Arison was her name, the fact that she owned a bank (which she has since sold), that she had an organization called Essence of Life, and that her late father's burial plot was very close to where my own parents were buried.

Over the years, I had passed Shari's father's grave whenever I visited the grave of my parents. In retrospect, I can only wonder if this was an early sign hinting at our future relationship?

Oh yeah, and I also knew that she was rich!

This was a potpourri of partial information which, in truth, painted a very inaccurate portrait of who Shari really was. But, as I didn't really know her at that time, this was not of much importance to me.

A week after the phone call, we met in Shari's office.

I sat on the sofa, my heart pounding. I wasn't sure why I was there. I was afraid Shari might ask me to channel with her father. I am not always able to connect with every soul with whom I am asked to connect, and the possibility that she might want me to try, put me under a bit of unwelcome stress. In spite of that fear, I was still happy to be there.

On my way to the meeting, I had felt a great sense of excitement, an excitement I could not quite understand. Perhaps it had something to do with the fact that I had felt a powerful connection to Shari even before meeting her. Many thoughts raced in my head:

Well, of course you're excited. This is Shari Arison we're talking about, a woman of influence, as they say. But there was another, a contradictory voice, that said, no, that isn't why you're feeling so excited.

I don't normally get excited by simple things like meeting someone who has read and liked my book. I didn't know exactly what to think. My emotions were jumbled and turbulent, but, even still, the feeling was actually quite pleasant.

Shari welcomed me with a smile. She was dressed in an elegant, meticulous, yet also modest fashion. She reached out her hand, wordlessly inviting me to enter and take a seat on the sofa. I looked around. The light that came through the large windows, filtered by the vegetation on the balcony, created a special and comfortable atmosphere.

Shari's desk was directly in front of me. On the wall beside it hung several family pictures. I felt a sense both of formality and a feeling of home. As Shari sat on the sofa next to me, I instantly felt a powerful rapport that I am still unable to put into words. I recognized that there was something about this connection that was, at the time, incomprehensible, but would be made clear to me in the future. The speed and the intensity involved were not things I had previously experienced.

In general, I love people a lot, but, normally, it takes some time for me to make a real connection. Feeling so quickly the intimacy that I did then, with a person I did not actually know, was not something that usually happened to me. Sometime later I discovered that Shari had felt the same way.

The first time we met, it was as if a spark of electricity passed between us! I felt that some mutual healing was taking hold of us both, something inexplicable, something which defied explanation, but could be felt in the body.

As it turned out, Shari had not invited me to her office to do channeling. She began by telling me how it was that she had come across my book, "Letters from Heaven."

I was on a business trip, looking into various projects, and a director of one of my publicly held companies gifted me your book. I thanked him as he explained, "You've been telling me about these things for years, and I could never understand what you were talking about. Having read this book, though, I think I understand you a little better." What he said intrigued me, so I went home and began reading it. I finished the book in two days and admired the simple, precise way you have of expressing things, always at eye-level. These were things I had always known, but you put them into language that anyone can understand.

I told myself that I simply had to meet you, but I did not immediately act on that feeling. My personal Facebook account is connected to the content of various spiritual organizations in Israel and abroad, and, suddenly, an ad promoting your book popped up on my page! I told myself it must surely be an indication that I needed to get a move on, but, again, I did not act on it to contact you. It was only after these ads popped up a few more times that I said, "That's it, Shari, the universe is trying to tell you something. Come on, reach out and contact her." It was then that I asked my staff to arrange a meeting between us.

As I listened to Shari, my mind began to fill with questions. What was this strangeness I was feeling? And what is the nature of this unusual connection? I just didn't know. There was a new energy I couldn't explain, a powerful force of mutual influence flowing between us. At that particular second, I was unable to understand what that force was and why it was there.

It was only long moments later that my inner turbulence began to subside, allowing me to be fully present at the meeting. This turned out to be the first meeting of many. In all of them, we simply sat and talked about our lives with candid openness, discussing the things we believed in. The more I learned about her daily life, her views, her way of connecting to herself, and who she is, the more I felt that there was so much more she would give—that I could get so much from her—not just me, everyone!

I realized that Shari was much more than a successful businesswoman. Thanks to her wealth there was so much good she could do in the world; so many ways for her to act to exert her positive influences. From this very first meeting, it was clear to me that Shari was motivated by a genuine and authentic desire, a true aspiration, to improve the world. I sensed her wish to help. I felt her genuine sense of distress caused by "the pain and suffering of humanity."

I was very surprised, because I had been misled by the mental image I had of Shari. I expected someone as successful as she to be very different from me, else she couldn't have reached the status that she had reached. I expected to find in her a powerful drive for success; a desire for even more status. I guess that I even expected to find in her a degree of forcefulness. I found none of those things!

It was more than that. During the course of this first conversation, I discovered a great deal about the wondrous journey she had undertaken in her search to find herself; in her efforts to tread the right path. Her ability to speak about things at "eye-level," derived from her personal experiences—not from the condescending attitude I had expected from a woman of her status—deeply moved me.

It was as soon as during that very first meeting, without comprehending why or how, that I knew we would write a book together. Shari felt this too, but neither of us knew what the book would be about. There were many questions racing through my mind. It would take time before the mists began to clear and the answers were revealed to me.

Even then, at that first meeting, I somehow knew the connection between us was no coincidence. Happily, Shari felt the same way.

Today, it is completely clear to me that Nurit and I share a mutual mission. We both grow, develop, understand more, and help one another to realize, each in her own way, the true mission of her soul.

I know that Shari has a vast mission to fulfill in this world, and I sense that it is a lot like my own, to share knowledge

*and life experiences with others. To help everyone, or at least
as many people as possible, dare to be who they truly are.*

*Sitting on the sofa in her brightly lit and pleasantly com-
fortable office, I saw the person she truly was—is!—the family pictures on the walls and in the bookcase at one end of
the room, and the area dedicated to business discussions and
conversation at the other.*

*I felt that Shari was comprised of many things, and that
she had somehow managed to combine all of the parts into a
harmonious whole. I was very interested to hear and understand how she had succeeded in achieving that. I wanted her
to show me the path that had led to her success and to reveal
the insights she had gained from the various experiences in
her life.*

*It was important that I understand her way because I felt
there was a great gift hidden within her—for me and for us
all. I wanted to understand what motivated her and how she
operated, because these were the ways that had brought her
to such significant success. They are the things I believed
then, and still do today, would help the rest of us to gain similar success. I am not merely referring to material success.
I am more interested in the level of mental tranquility and
balance Shari has attained; the inner peace she experiences,
her pleasant ways.*

*One day, while Shari was relating something to me from
her world, I realized one of her characteristics I find so en-
ticing. It is the clarity of the way in which she operates—the
belief she has that each of us has his or her own uniqueness;
that once we recognize that uniqueness, and who we really
are, worlds will open to us.*

*And so, the book you are holding was born. For me, it is a
guidebook for all of us about how to be more at peace with
who we are; to understand who we are and bring ourselves*

to the world in the best possible way, not just for our own benefit, but for that of the whole world.

These days, the inability to achieve self-fulfillment causes much pain and frustration, while self-fulfillment generates much happiness and joy. I think that what I wish for most of all, is that we, all of us, can live in a state of self-fulfillment. Those are some of the reasons why I am so happy to be a part of this book, and to share with Shari, her hope:

That this book Nurit and I have created together will help you, dear reader, to fulfill the destiny of your soul. That such self-fulfillment can happen only when you know the answer to the question, Who am I really?

Is There Only
One Way Leading
to Growth?

I was sitting beside Shari on the sofa in her office. This had become very familiar to me over the past few months Shari was speaking, her eyes sparkling:

The most important thing is for people to realize that the lifespan of this book is endless! It is a book to which one can, and should, go back, time and again.

What do you mean?

This is a book that holds something new for every reader with each new reading. It has so much food for thought, so many questions we can ask ourselves. You might take a notebook and write down the answers to its questions. Then, a year or more later, reread those answers to see how much they have changed. Amazingly enough, they do change—sometimes completely.

I thought to myself how profoundly concepts in my life had changed in recent years thanks to the processes I had undergone; and, indeed, I am still going through.

In any given period, things change. I happen occasionally to re-read things I wrote years before and I am amazed to see where I had been back then, compared to where I am today. I am now in a completely different place.

While the feelings are the same feelings, I was sad then. Indeed, there are some situations that still make me sad today. which is fine, but the story involving the same feeling and the way I relate to it are completely different.

When the story changes, one's understanding becomes different, which is why you also behave and feel differently. The story itself is irrelevant. It is merely a trigger. The feeling is the same. What changes is the speed with which you come to understand that feeling and release it.

So, a person who reads this book and answers the questions in it will know themselves better and come to understand who they truly are?

Yes, but there is no one correct way of doing this. One of the most significant things I believe in is pluralism— the recognition that there is no single correct way. I've always known this, and I constantly come back to it. Many of the teachers I studied with believe that theirs is the only true way, the only correct path that will lead to what we seek in life.

The Essence of Life organization which I founded, is based on the principle that there is no single, true way. On the contrary, there are countless ways of attaining what is right for each person, and each person needs to do what is right for themselves. What is right and suitable for me, isn't necessarily right and suitable for you.

The emotional approach is most suitable for some people, while others are better suited to a rational, intellectual approach. Still others will best find their way through a sensual or experiential path.

We are each built differently. The moment one realizes this, then there is no more "good" or "bad." There is no more "right" or "wrong." Instead, there are different shades of different ways, creating a variety of different paths, from which we each can choose the one most suitable. Each person must examine what is suitable for them; what resonates and rings true for them.

It is just like music. There are many different types of music—from classical to hip hop. Each of us connects with one style, or maybe more.

We especially love to hear someone making "our kind" of music; the kind we connect with. It is exactly the same with spirituality and personal development. The moment we begin to listen to ourselves, we realize that, even if we are offered, say, a most wonderful workshop, if something inside us feels that this workshop is just not right for us, then it must not be right for us.

On the other hand, you might recommend a different workshop to me, or a book, a lecture, or a certain method, and it will be the right one. There are no absolutes. What feels right for me today may not feel that way one year, or ten years, from now. It is important to remain constantly connected—inwardly—to understand what is right for us at any given time.

In this way, we can develop. We can become empowered. We can experience the growth to reach a better world. At first for each of us and our own selves, and then for each of us and the others close beyond (our family and our inner circle), and then, to resonate out into the wider circle that is the world.

I was greatly touched by Shari's words, for I, too, believe that there is no single true way—that we each need to seek out and create our individual path, the one most suitable for us. Furthermore, what is right for us today, may not feel that way tomorrow. Some people study with me for many years, while others come just for a single workshop or course and go on their way.

How did you come to the idea of pluralism, Did you believe from the beginning that there are many different ways that lead to growth?

I think that all through my life I have been "tasting" different "flavors" of personal development—from the conventional to the spiritual—many of which I elaborated upon in my first book, Birth: When the Spiritual and the Material Come Together.

I have always been interested in religions and different cultures. I may be Jewish, but I very much enjoy visiting churches. Wherever I travel around the world, it is always very important for me to become familiar with the culture, art, cuisine, and the local flavor of that place. I think that this is something that was a part of me for as long as I have lived, but I must have been unable to recognize this until I finally came to the understanding that, in order to reach a state of peace with the world, we each must first reach a state of peace with ourselves, and our environment.

Once I had come to that conclusion, I was able to see a better world, one which many people call "utopian," but one that I strongly believe is possible to achieve—a world in which people respect and love each other and are able to develop, all in harmony, achieving growth and perpetual creation.

But, in order for this to happen, we must each first find our way within our own individual inner world. That is because the external world reflects the inner world of each of us. I don't know how much time all this will take—I wish it would come to fulfilment and be realized in my lifetime—in ours—but it could take a hundred, or even two-hundred, years.

Shari's words strengthened me; they eased the inner criticism I subjected myself to. Invariably, that self-criticism would say to me, "Try to engage people to stay with you over a long period of time." Obviously, I would love it if everyone were to study with me over extended periods of time, but there is a powerful voice inside me that tells me that this would be right for some individuals, but less so for others. Every individual has the inherent ability to discover what is right for them to progress and develop, and for each it is a little different.

How Can We Be Attentive to Ourselves?

The more I got to know Shari, the more I realized how true she is to herself, but more importantly true to the values she believes in. It became important that I find the answer to a question that had been on my mind. How was Shari able to combine the demanding and (to my opinion) often harsh business world with all her diverse philanthropic undertakings, for the good of all, to change and improve things. I asked her how she manages to steer her way through all of the different voices that proclaim the judgement and criticism that surround her.

For me, navigating my way in the business world is no different to how I find my way around any of the other circles of my life. It is important for me to work with an inner moral compass and to always remain true to myself. I am attentive to myself and to others. It is important for me that the people around me bring their individual truth and find a harmonious bridge.

One of the tools I use when the answer, or the way, is not clear to me, is to be attentive to various signs. People often think that things are coincidental and do not pay any attention to them, but I am very open to all of the signs that come through me.

If I have a question, the type of question and reflection we all have occasionally, about a specific deal, or about my career, about relationships, the family, children, about personal growth, about what I want or don't want, what is precise and what isn't, whether something is right or not, a mistake or not—any of these or any other questions or thoughts—I ask myself and the universe the relevant questions, and I then open myself to the signs that appear to me along the way.

The sign may come in the form of a book I'm reading, a commercial billboard, or a word someone uses in the first sentence I hear when I turn on the television. The signs can come in a variety of forms. We just need to be aware of them. Everything is inside of us. We know better than anyone else what is right for ourselves; what is exact and fitting for us in regard to our health, livelihood, relationships, or family—every aspect of our lives.

Sometimes, when we are exploring/asking/deliberating, the universe hears our voice. We merely need to be clear about what we have asked, what our dilemma is, and then remain attentive to what the universe provides to us.

I identified with Shari's words. I, too, feel that I am playing a game of road signs with the universe. I ask for signs to guide my next steps to provide confidence for the direction I am taking. They come in various ways, but for someone as skeptical as I am, it is often hard to rely on the answers I receive.

Unlike Shari, I have been afraid to trust the universe. Not that I did not receive signs while starting out on my way as a channeler. On the contrary, the signs were always there, but I was afraid to accept them. I thought that perhaps what I saw, felt, or heard was a coincidence; that perhaps, because I was seeking the answer, I was inventing the connection I wished for. But alongside doubt, there was also a side that insisted that I not ignore the signs I was getting. I sensed that there was truth in them.

I began to ask for signs that the sign I had received was true. I sought additional reinforcements, and these have, indeed, come. The signs I have received in the physical world are among the most empowering things imaginable. I cannot possibly convince myself that I have made them up (one of the most common concerns of those who experience channeling) when there are tangible things taking place right in front of my eyes.

Still, in the beginning, I often found myself confused. There was something inside me that actually hoped that I would prove to myself that this was nonsense, a pure invention of mine. I felt that life would be simpler that way, without the need to explain myself to anyone who failed to understand.

Another part of me sought confirmation for this inner sense; that there was truth there for me, a truth that would make my life brighter and simpler. So, I went on seeking empowering signs. Every time I was unable to provide a logical explanation for something that was demonstrated by reality, I was further empowered. I was able to believe and trust a little bit more.

Finally, I let go of this struggle and gave myself to my own inner truth. I continue to be surprised by the precision with which the messages and guidance come. I am still bound to the familiar logic from my past, but I no longer let it stop me.

I admire the faith that has accompanied Shari throughout her life and I asked her to tell me about her process of personal development.

I think I've always believed in the adage: When the student is ready, the teacher will appear. Whenever I have had a desire to develop in a specific direction, no matter whether it was spiritual or material; whenever I was ready and relayed to the universe that I wanted to learn about X or Y, the right answer presented itself to me. It might have come as a person, a book, a lecture, a workshop, a method, or one of a million other things. If I "relayed" this desire to the universe and something came back but I failed to pay attention or listen to it, I missed an opportunity. True, the same opportunity might present itself again in some other way, but, normally, it arrives as if someone had hit you in the head.

If you remain attentive, you will receive both the answers and the "how to go about it" method: how to develop, how to implement, how to grow, how to nurture, and, of course, what you should do. What surprises and moves me, is that when we remain open we always learn something, and we find ways in which to develop.

To give you an example, many years ago I studied "mindfulness." After many years of experiencing a great many methods of meditation, I realized that, for me, mindfulness was just the right fit. I practiced it every day for years.

Recently, at work, as part of "The Doing Good Model," it was suggested we hold a mindfulness course. When I noted that we had already conducted such a course in the company, I was informed that, since then, many new employees had joined us and we should teach the technique again. We brought in a new instructor to deliver the course and I found myself surprised after years of practicing, that I was able to learn new things—and that these things brought me into an even deeper connection with myself.

Shari's words prompted me to have additional thoughts.

No matter how many years a person studies, their realization that they may still have a lot to learn, and that they should be willing to learn from anyone who happens to cross their path, isn't obvious. But, when Shari quoted the saying, "When the student is ready, the teacher will appear," a judgmental thought immediately came into my mind: Oh, well, that's easy for you to say when you're Shari Arison and can get any teacher to come to you with a single phone call!

Having thought that, I immediately felt that I was doing her an injustice. After all, not every person who has the means to do so will choose to seek out the right teacher. Shari's need to find her "right path" was very much like my own. I thought about the many programs of study in which I had participated and I felt my heart overflowing with joy for having found the right ways to invest in the means to advance myself.

It was at that moment, too, that I realized that, by continuing to view Shari as "Shari Arison" I was also doing an injustice to myself. I was creating a gap between us in the field of spiritual study and growth that did not actually exist; a gap that prevented me from acquiring learning by observing the path that Shari had taken.

I was silent for a moment. Shari shared that silence with me. Thoughts that embarrassed me came into my mind. I could see the path that Shari had taken. I could hear the pain that sometimes came into her voice. Clearly, she had had her share of difficult challenges in life. This moved me and entered my heart. But then, without my meaning it to do so, I suddenly saw in her, too, the icon who lived in a different world from mine.

Was it truly so? Was her world really so different from my own? Or, was this a prejudice rooted in my mind; one preventing me from truly listening to her?

Because I had a deep gut-feeling that Shari was actually sharing her truth with me—sharing the path she had taken without any attempt to beautify it, or to wrap it in a pretty box—I felt I was missing some of its essence. I, who was so proud of my openness, of my willingness and wish to accept each-and-every person, to listen to their personal stories and learn from them at eye-level, suddenly discovered that it felt much more comfortable for me to do that with people who were "my equals" (or those I considered to be my equals).

That made it extremely challenging for me to remain open and attentive to Shari, because I was unable to bridge the material difference I felt existed between us.

It was at that moment that I determined to try to put aside this sense of a gap between us, and listen to Shari, the person, rather than to "Shari Arison, the icon."

I directed my gaze back at Shari and asked her how she knew when the time had come to make a change; to change a teacher, for example, or to try a new learning method. Shari smiled and answered.

To change is also to be attentive to yourself. I have many times studied a certain method and exhausted it. I felt that I understood its principle. People often latch onto a certain teacher, turn someone into a guru, or cling to a certain method or way. I, personally, do not believe in that. I believe that God, the Creation, manifests in all the spectrum of shades and forms. So, if I study only one form, I prevent myself from experiencing the others. That is why I am always very attentive to myself. When I see I've reached a point of completion, I part ways with it—sometimes in a single moment. Sometimes it takes longer, because it isn't easy to part ways with something good, but then I am open again to the next thing, or the next desire. I stand ready to face the next question, and I am open to whatever comes.

I think that this is something that has been with me my whole life. I understand it today and I have the ability to explain it with words, but it wasn't always like that. There was a time when I was unable to explain it, but I still conducted myself that way.

I nodded empathetically. I, too, feel that there is much exciting knowledge to be explored in the world, and many more ways than just one to do so. That is why it is so important for me to try and experience different things—to find what is truly suitable for me.

I have been in situations in life when it was extremely difficult to part ways with a teacher I studied with. I often felt that a certain teacher had abilities and knowledge I lacked, and only if I continued to cling to them would I be able to experience growth. But, more accurately, this was because I had turned the teacher into something more significant than myself. It is truly painful to look back on; to realize how easily we diminish ourselves and give our inherent power to someone else. We come to think that they may hold the answers we lack, or we hope that a certain way will "save" us.

Today, I realize that true power is in the hands of each and every one of us. That true power lies in being attentive, in learning, and in being able to recognize when something is no longer suitable or fitting for us.

That is why Shari's words moved me so much. It seems that she knew she should stay with a certain teacher only so long as she could learn and receive from that person. And, the moment it was no longer suitable for her, she moved on. I tried to understand how she did this.

Are you saying that over the years you have gradually learned to listen to your gut instinct? Is that what has guided your way?

Yes, many times I did fail to listen to my gut and, in doing so, I actually learned a lot from not listening. Many times I would feel something, but I would be unable to decipher it. Back then, I would listen to the external noises; to what other people thought, to what the media said. That all led me to a bad place, and I received my fair share of hard blows because of it; exactly the kind of strikes you get when you fail to listen to yourself. And then, just as a GPS application does, I recalculated my route.

Over time, I learned to fine tune those feelings. Today, if I feel something in my gut, even if I do not understand it, I will still listen to it, but realize that something about it is not right for me. While everything might look wonderful on the outside . . . still . . . I have this gut feeling that something isn't sitting quite right. Today I listen to these gut feelings, and I find that doing so is true and useful in all aspects of life—between me and myself, and between me and others; in family life, and in business.

I paused again to think.

One of the things that characterizes many of the people who come to me, and possibly that characterizes most "rational" people in the western world, is the desire to cling to facts—to tangible proof—to know what is right or not with the same clarity that is used to solve a mathematical equation. We have been taught to "think rationally," to analyze, and to draw conclusions based on the facts.

Feelings, on the other hand, are thought to be not rooted in fact. It is why many of us treat our feelings as something imprecise, perhaps even invented. We ignore our emotions, thereby missing vital information.

Today, I realize that the gut feelings—my intuition, the feelings that surge in me when things happen, are all real, and are as tangible as facts. The actuality is that the feelings are invariably mine. It is why they reflect my truth with better precision. We have been taught not to trust our feelings because they are confusing, but when we ignore the feelings that arise in us, we may act in ways not right for us. As Shari said, it is extremely important to listen to our feelings. We may not always be able to immediately understand the message behind them, but the more we develop our attentiveness, the more things become clear and guide us on our path.

When we listen to external noises and ignore our inner selves, our body speaks to us. It can take such forms as a headache, a stomachache, or extreme tiredness. If we want to connect with our inner truth, we must begin to listen to our feelings and to what is going on in our body, because it gives us signs.

It is just like that, I thought to myself. Our bodies talk to us all the time. Actually, a large proportion of the messages we receive come to us in the form of physical sensations. Truly, many times when I have ignored a voice inside me, I have felt some sort of physical pain—a headache or a neck pain; sometimes more. Today, whenever I feel discomfort in my body, I seek to understand what that discomfort wants to tell me.

When we act against the inner feelings inside us, we are always sorry later; and sometimes we get hurt because of it. I asked Shari to elaborate about the "blows" she has taken in her life.

Oh, I've had more than a few of those, Shari said with a shy smile. I've suffered many hard blows throughout my life. It's all a matter of perspective, of course. I can speak in broader terms, but it is like in any interpersonal relationships—romantic relations, parenthood, friendships. Looking outside of yourself, you look at what the other person wants. If I do this, it will upset him. Or, if I do that, I will hurt him. Or, If I do this other thing, then . . . .

Will he love me? I interjected from my own world.

. . . then there will be criticism. And I don't feel like being criticized! So, we continue to think about external reactions.

The energy I have invited is an energy of criticism, which is why criticism is the reaction I get. But, once you begin to look within and ask yourself, "Wait, is that the right thing for me to give this person, X or Y? Yes! Because I really do feel like giving it. I enjoy giving to others, whatever the reaction might be." If I get a positive reaction, great; if it's negative, well, that kind of reaction belongs to the person who gave it, but I will be at peace with myself.

Or, if something bothers me and I want to talk about it, I might find myself in a situation invoking two types of reaction that are completely contrary to each other. The first involves setting out everything I think, angrily. The justification for this would be that I was simply expressing my truth, no matter how the other person receives it. The second kind of reaction would have to do with fear or avoidance. No, I won't say anything because it will cause conflict, and I don't want to be in a conflict.

Having gone through a process of self-observation, self-work, and growth, I can speak my truth from a quiet place of comfort without hurting the person I am with. It is also important, however, that I keep my eyes open and be aware of the state I am in and where I am. If I am agitated and upset, it is not the right time to talk. It is better if I wait until I am more relaxed. But, it is also important to see where the other person is. Sometimes we want to voice something that the other person is not willing or yet ready to hear. In such cases, it is better to wait until the other person is ready, and we can then have a constructive conversation.

A sense of curiosity had wakened in me, and, to be honest, so had the prying part of me. Shari had shared a weakness that I was personally familiar with. I was very interested to hear more about the specifics of what she had gone through. I asked her to give me examples from her life; to share actual incidents that had happened, to help me understand better. She presented me the difference between us. This time, I knew the difference was real.

Nearly every person I might mention to you is a public figure. The companies I had are well known. While I am willing to share with you my world and what has happened to me within it, I cannot expose specific situations nor mention individuals by name. It would not be right to do so.

I was a little shocked for a moment. I had not truly stopped to consider this. The stories taken from my own life, and the experiences I might talk about, are not related to well-known people. What difference would the particular school I had studied at make? Which lecturer I had had an argument with? The learning experience is what would matter. But, when "Shari Arison" is the one doing the telling, the specifics suddenly become very interesting. Who did that happen with? And where? We are all familiar with many of the people with whom she has had dealings and relationships. When Shari is doing the telling, it can become gossip. When I am doing the telling, it's just a personal story.

It is amusing to think that I actually have much greater freedom to share the details of my life's story with the world. My husband, my children, and my friends are not familiar to you. They are simply background characters. Furthermore, I think it is easier for you to believe me, because you understand in advance that my story is presented merely to illustrate a point. However, when "Shari Arison" tells the story, the recipient's mood may be different—it can be more judgmental, perhaps even doubtful. One can't help but look for some hidden subtext in the story. I assume this is just a part of being human. The moment a certain image has been associated in one's mind with a specific person, we seek the things that will cement that image even more strongly.

I understood why Shari wasn't willing to talk about personal examples that involve other people, and I respect her for it. Still, I asked her to elaborate more about the "blows" she had suffered.

Such a blow can come when you are in love with someone and that person leaves you. A blow can be struck if your health suddenly deteriorates. A hard blow occurs when you give your heart and soul to your business and the results aren't exactly what you had imagined and wanted. There are all sorts of hardships.

Some people suffer a hardship and are never able to recover from it. Others do not even try; or they make accusations, looking to place blame elsewhere. Others suffer a blow and say, okay, this has happened to teach me something. What have I missed? What have I failed to understand?

Even when you have learned and you understand, it does not mean that you have finished studying. You are still in the process of study—you can go still deeper—learning one more layer, one more angle. It can be the same lesson coming from different angles and different depths. Then you can be simply attentive to what the world brings you, to what you are going through, and what you are able to learn from it.

Once again, a thought similar to one that had occurred to me earlier passed through my mind. What? Shari Arison— afraid of being criticized? I chased that thought away immediately. I had heard so much vulnerability in her voice. Why, then, was it so hard for me to let go of my preconceived image of Shari-the-public-figure and listen to Shari-the-person (of whom I was growing fonder with every passing minute)?

I thought about how I, too, was afraid of being criticized, afraid of not being loved. I have tried to make this fear go away for years. I felt angry. How could it be that I was involved in such a significant process of self-development, yet I was still so intimidated every time I felt I might have hurt someone, or that I might have done something wrong. I wanted so much for that feeling to pass, to go away. I wanted to be free of it.

In one of the conversations that I had had with one of my spiritual guides, he told me, "You human beings are taught to want to 'fix' the faults in yourselves. The way we see it from beyond, is that they aren't faults at all, but personality structures. The soul brings with it certain personality traits. There are traits that you must accept in yourselves and learn how to live with them in the best possible way; in the same way that an especially short person realizes that is their genetic makeup and they have to learn to live with that situation and make the best of it. The same can be said about accepting specific personality traits that a person possesses. Once you stop fighting with who you are and learn to lead an active life with it, you will not only become much more successful, you will also feel much better about yourself."

The spiritual guide's words seemed so logical to me that I have embraced them ever since. While it does not always work, I realize that my greatness is not measured by how much I succeed in erasing certain character traits I have, but by how well I learn to live peacefully with them.

I was able to see that Shari wasn't different from me. She also had certain traits that she liked less, certain things she wanted to release. I suddenly realized how brave she had been to act in spite of her fears, and recognized the way in which she had dared to be different to find the path most suitable for herself.

"The message I take from your words," I said thoughtfully to Shari, "is that you have allowed yourself to walk down 'other' paths. That you have learned about life through your personal experiences. Sometimes you were shy, and other times you were daring—prominent. You have waded your

way through experience; learned your lessons not from this or that teacher, but from life itself." As I spoke, I was aware that my words blended a statement with a question.

As for the personality structure, even what appears to us as personality structure can be made to change and develop. We grow in a certain way and sometimes believe that it is a personality trait. However, this is something that can be changed with enough will and determination.

I grew up in an atmosphere full of very negative thoughts, but I wanted to be positive, and I worked on it, step by step. Today, everyone who meets me marvels at how optimistic I always am. They do not realize how much work it has taken to make that change. And yes, with me, everything passes through first-hand experience. Every single thing in my life, in all areas of life, it has been a first-hand experience, both outward and inward, both flesh and soul. Throughout my adult life I have realized that whenever I work on myself, it reflects outwardly in my undertakings as a mother, a businesswoman, a philanthropist, and as an author. I have developed in all of the circles of my life. I have connected inwardly, and then, the endeavor has grown and expanded in the physical, external world as well."

What do you mean by ". . . work on myself?"

I went through a lot of emotional development, spiritual development, meditation, and introspection. I studied various methods, studying with different teachers, and I developed appreciably with each method and with each teacher. I became more intimately familiar with myself. I received various impressions, opened my heart, and I developed compassion. These are small examples, because how can you describe all of forty years of spiritual work?

It is customary to think that being true to yourself is contrary to being attentive to others, but there is a difference between egotism and self-caring, and the difference is vast. It would be more precise to say that I am connected to myself—deeply connected to my inner-self—to the divine spark in me, to the place where we are all one, all connected. It is that place where an action taken by any one of us affects all of us—for good or for bad. I am connected to my emotions, my heart, my thoughts, my general state of being, and, yes, to my gut too. We all need to listen and discern the voices inside us; to hear them all and to choose what we want.

Take fear, for example. In the past, fear had been a tremendously important emotion. It protected us from attackers and predators. It was vital for our survival. It had a reason. We no longer need this protection so much today, yet fear still sometimes drives us.

So, you need to be aware of it, understand that it comes from something very ancient that was greatly useful once—and then let it go. Because today it makes us feel small, and it stops us. You can let go of it and choose courage instead. That is just a brief example.

The ego doesn't listen, but when you listen to yourself, you do what is right and proper for you, along with providing a lot of care and love for others. This does not mean that others should need to accept what you are doing, or even feel good about what you are doing, but as long as you mean well, as long as you do not intend to do harm, as long as you listen to yourself and always keep your heart open and loving, you will live in peace with it.

How Does One Learn from the Path Taken?

I agreed with Shari that being true to oneself is the most important thing. I was taught that I must always think about others first, and about myself after—and then only if and when there was any room left in there for me. But really, there is never any room left.

I think most people I meet never stop to think what is right for them; and even if they do, the fear of what people will say, the concern that they might hurt someone, stops them from being the person they would really like to be.

I am forever filled with a sense of missed opportunity or a lack of self-actualization when I am not attentive to myself. It is possible to do both; to think of others, while not giving up on oneself.

Just as Shari had said, it really is simply a matter of listening to yourself. However, I am sad to say that the old fears often drive me and I am not always able to act in the way I want to. I am always newly surprised by how strong that fear of hurting others is—so strong that it makes me prefer not to act in a way that might cause such harm. What

I have realized over the years is that this fear is actually a self-prevention; that the fear of saying my piece, of being wholly present, is what might cause the most harm.

And, I have learned that my fear can be felt by others. When I diminish myself, I send a subliminal message to others that not being free is the right thing to be.

Rereading what I have previously written I realize how wrong is the set of beliefs on which I was raised. No matter what I do, there will always be someone who may not like it. I truly do not know what is right for others. Any attempt to guess that or try to act in a way that I think would be right for them would not only be incorrect, it would also be impossible.

I agree that the most important inner barometer to use is how peacefully we live with our past actions and choices. It is perfectly fine to make mistakes, and perfectly fine not to know things. It is alright to be afraid. I know that so long as I am connected with love, and with an open heart, everything will work out.

Sometimes I feel that I really want to be at the next stage already—to feel that all fears and doubt are behind me—to be able to stop checking and measuring everything that I am doing all of the time. There! I am being judgmental right now. Enough! I will return to connect with the heart. I want to admire the path I have taken. I want to enjoy the place I have come to rather than always to just see what needs to be done next.

I felt a pang of jealousy of Shari. It seemed to me as if she was really truly at peace with herself.

I wanted to learn from her how to be more attentive to myself, to my gut instincts. I, too, have developed inner instincts that I use to help others, to do things related to myself and my work, but when it comes to myself, I am not as daring in listening to them. It sounded to me like Shari was using her gut instincts when it had to do with herself, with others, and with business-related matters. That said, I was really interested in learning how she managed to combine both her own well-being and the well-being of the rest of the world.

As far as I'm concerned, the way I see things, all my undertakings must be for the benefit of all. And that means, whatever it is, it should benefit me as well. In the past, I used to sacrifice myself for the sake of others. Today, I understand that everything I do has to be a win-win situation. In other words, any undertaking I engage in has got to be for my benefit as well as for others. If it is something that benefits my businesses, then it should also benefit my employees and the community, the country, and the environment. It has to be like that on every level.

Shari's words reinforced my belief, my understanding, that it is not right to think only of others. To hear from Shari that this same sentiment also drove her business endeavors genuinely moved me. I felt that Shari had a genuine need to change things, to do good in the world, because it was clear that she had already had her fair share of successes and accomplishments. Yet, some inward force motivated her to go on to do the next thing. Where does she draw this energy from? How does she not get tired?

I think that any person connected to their soul will be in continuous motion, always creating the next thing, because creation is something that is always creating, and always changing. And I think I am simply connected to my soul and it is the reason why I am always in the process of creation. It's simple. I once would have maybe used the term "an artist's heart," but, today, I think we each have the divine spark within us. That divine spark is creation, and creation has to do with always creating; it neither stops nor ends. Creation never ceases.

Shari's words made me think about myself again. It's true, I thought in my heart, when I am connected to the change I would like to bring to the world, with following the path that is right for me, I always have the strength and the will to act. It is only when I drift away from my truth, out of fear or a lack of attentiveness, that I stop. I get lost. And then I have no strength to act.

What was the first project you completed that was meaningful for you? I asked. I was very curious to learn how it had all begun. Shari laughed.

Wow, my first project? I don't know. Do we really want to talk about me at age thirteen?

I wasn't entirely sure whether she was joking or she meant she actually had begun so young. Once again, she seemed to belong to a world completely different from my own— someone born with a "silver spoon in her mouth." Then I remembered! That wasn't true. Her father had become rich when Shari was almost thirty years old. The difference I had created between us now faded, and cleared for me a different path to curiosity and smile-filled admiration.

I was surprised. Had she really started as early as age thirteen? I then recognized my need to put tags onto everything, to define her actions in a way that would make it easier for me to understand her. Perhaps that came from my tendency to maintain that gap between us?

In certain respects, it was convenient for me to believe that Shari was able to do things I wasn't able to, simply because of the conditions in her life. It offered me an affirmation that my place in life was fine. I chuckled to myself. I was actually doing it yet again!—putting Shari up and putting myself down.

On one hand, when we were having an intimate conversation, drinking coffee together, she was Shari. Just Shari. We would talk about our children, our work, our fears, our dilemmas, as genuine equals. On the other hand, she might then tell me that something was about to happen in one of her businesses; something that she could not share because she was legally forbidden from doing so. Once again I would then see only "Shari Arison, the icon."

However, I began to feel that perhaps that reaction was all right. That I could view her in that way at certain times, and in a different way at others. Because she is both real and an icon!

She has something that is unique and different from me. This is fine, even as she shares many similarities with me. Perhaps it was time to connect the two images of Shari inside me, to form a single joined image rather than an either/or.

I realized that I had better do this, not because it was or was not fair to Shari, but because it was not fair to me. While it is true that Shari had had opportunities that I had not, she could have taken these in many directions. She did not have to search for ways to contribute to society, nor to constantly act to achieve personal development. I realized that if I truly wanted to gain and learn from the path she walked, I had better start viewing Shari as a single being, a multifaceted person, with each facet being a part of her whole self. Shari smiled.

I really did start at age thirteen. I worked at "Chicken Unlimited," a fast-food restaurant. I fried burgers, chicken, and fries. I packaged the food in bags and I served customers for the ability to have some pocket money.

I, later, volunteered to join the Israeli army, and then, after my military service, I returned to the United States to work in my family's company. I worked in each of the company's departments, starting from entry-level positions, allowing me to slowly and gradually become familiar with every aspect of the business from the inside.

I studied to be a travel agent. At one point, I even worked as a travel agent outside the family company until my children were born. Around age twenty-seven, after I had had three of my four children, I was asked to form a family foundation to accept donations.

To learn about, and to understand this new field, I arranged to meet with representatives from the major foundations in the area where I lived. I volunteered to serve as a board member for many non-profit organizations, and I returned to the family company to join its board of directors as well.

Even without detailing my path in philanthropic activities, I can say that in all my endeavors, in every area, I have always combined a process of learning and self-development, leading with vision and strategy, to bring the values of the organization or business to a better place; one of growth, of values, of caring, along with its financial, social, and environmental gains.

In business, I think the first thing that guided me at the start of my journey, was the need and the wish to learn how a large organization works.

While Shari had been speaking, to try to fathom her methods of operation, I was attempting to put what she was saying in some sort of order in my head.

What I understand from what you are saying, I said, and I suppose, from your viewpoint, this is true of all of us—both small business owners and people who just want to fulfill something—is that to every new place you may go, you first observe and understand what it is that is going on there. Then you begin in other ways to study the place from all possible angles.

Yes. My friends have always said to me, "You, when you get into something, you go in deep." It isn't just in business, it's the same with spirituality. When I learn a new method, I delve deep into its depths. I make sure I don't just float around on the surface of things.

I tried to put into other words the way Shari did things. So, you actually learn what is happening in a certain place, within a business, let's say, a company, or a spiritual method, and only after you feel that you fully understand . . . . Shari finished my sentence for me.

Only then do I act. And, when I feel it has fulfilled itself for me, I move on.

I thought about myself again. About how many times I have not even tried to do something because I felt I didn't know how. How many times have I simply given up? And this isn't just me, it is often the way many of us act. Repeatedly.
When the path is unclear, we stop. I feel that most of us do not dare to act, or be willing to go down a certain path

because we don't know "how" to do it. "Being who you are" requires inner attentiveness and searching to understand what is truly important for us, what is right for us, and what our inner motivation is.

But, let's suppose I know who I am. Let's suppose that I even know what I want; that it is something different from what I have done up to today. However, I do not have even the first clue about how I should do it. In the past, feelings like that have stopped me from acting. I always searched the clear path to go down—and never have found it! There were always question marks. Would I succeed? Would it work? I was always intimidated.

When I listened to Shari talking about her first steps, I found, on one hand, that it inspired me and made me want to do great things. On the other, I knew I lacked her background, her experience, and, of course, her resources. What could I possibly take from her experiences?

Shari reminded me that she, too, did not have a clue at first and had known nothing when she started out. But, still, I was insistent in questioning on.

You need to sit with people who understand, so you can learn the language, she began.

Impatiently, I interjected, "Are you saying that I need to find a teacher? That we, each of us, need to find the one person who can help us understand? Someone who has the knowledge we require?"

Yes. You need to find someone who is expert in whatever you are seeking to do and learn that from him or her; gain a deeper understanding. But I do want to clarify that there are several types of learning; there is practical learning, like what I had to learn when I started out at a bank that was under my ownership back then. I wasn't even familiar with the terms they used, the banking language. I had to learn what banking is, how a bank works. That is an intellectual type of learning, knowledge you get from a teacher, like mathematics.

Then there is a different type of learning—soulful learning. It is learning to develop one's principles, to become connected to your own will, to understand where you want to get to, and to learn to accept various types of people. Soulful learning is a kind of learning that is assimilated in the body.

When I was first on the bank's board of directors, there were finance people among them who were enthusiastic about numbers. Numbers bored me, but I learned that numbers are important. I learned to appreciate the people I worked with, and I learned what I had and could offer to the business: vision, transformation, and a spiritual dimension.

You must learn on both of those levels. You need to combine the intellectual with the spiritual, using both information and actual experience. You must have your feet on the ground and your head in the vision. It is important to assimilate both these levels in life, not separate them. Allow them to coexist.

I immediately felt that that was the right way for everyone. I truly connected to learning. Even today, after finding my way in the world and doing what I love to do, I know that each change or business development needs time. There is time needed to learn the process, a time for me to study myself in this new field. You can never give up learning. It, alone, provides the precision we require to succeed.

Are Shari's methods suitable for all of us, despite the different conditions in all of our lives? Was I, again, missing something? But wait, I reminded myself. What had originally moved me while getting to know Shari was that she was doing only what she truly believes in. Does every successful businesswoman act in this way? I asked myself whether any individual who has received a fortune busies themselves in trying to better the world and profit in the way Shari does?

The answer was obvious and leapt instantly to my mind. Of course not!

I thought about Shari's job in the fast-food restaurant. Shari did not begin life with the proverbial silver spoon in her mouth, and, even later, nothing was given to her for no reason. She had to prove herself at each step of the way. I was pretty sure it wasn't that simple. So what is it that motivates her?

Taking into account everything you've told me about your early start, your difficulties, what gave you the strength to go on and make progress? Was it the fact that you engaged in the things that you believed in? That you acted, not out of knowledge, but out of a need to understand? Shari smiled and nodded.

Right. My life wasn't always easy. I had to prove myself and fight for my place. No matter what I did, there were always some who loved it, and others who didn't. This wasn't easy to accept, because I'm very sensitive. However, there is one thing that has always given me strength and led me all of my life—my belief in God, in my mission. My belief that we can create a better world, make a change, and that I, myself, can change things. It is a belief in my role in this world."

I believed in the world I saw inside myself. There were those who called me naïve, but I know, with a deep inner certainty, that we are capable of reaching a world that has love, unity, harmony, and abundance. The choice is ours, and I choose to do everything to bring myself, those around me, and the whole world, to this better place. That is still what drives and motivates me. But, it is very important to differentiate between authentic willpower and the ego. If it is the ego that drives you, it can take you to places that aren't necessarily positive.

I was filled with a strange feeling. In one way, I admired the way Shari operated. In the other way, doubt was blooming in me again. Was this how I, too, could act? Or perhaps, again, was it a unique path that only Shari could have taken because of her status?

At that moment, an insightful realization arose in me— and brought tears to my eyes. How easy it was for me to become emotional, listening to the stories of people who began their lives in a low place and then built themselves up with their very own hands . . . .

Even if those individuals had not always acted in accord with my own set of values, I still held a deep appreciation for them. I thought about the excitement and belief with which others listened to my own personal story—the story of how I built myself and my business.

I considered how much one's attitudes can change when we think that someone has not had to forge their own way, but, instead, has started out with a firm financial foundation, or a "business shortcut." In those cases, my appreciation for that person is often tinged with suspicion. No matter what that person does, my evaluation of them becomes judgmental.

Most of us are unable to look at someone in a truly pure and unbiased way. We are influenced by the person's background, by the media, and by the set of beliefs we hold. I wondered to what extent we allow our own selves to see ourselves in this pure way—to support who we truly are and to support our own actions without being judgmental.

I realized that there is a close connection between my willingness (anyone's willingness, actually) to see our own greatness, and our willingness to see the greatness in others, no matter who they are.

There is greatness in every being—courage, originality, wisdom—that we can learn from if we would only stop being judgmental. If I hadn't known that this was Shari Arison with whom I was sitting, wouldn't I have admired the path she had taken, perhaps even more; admired the way she had acted? Couldn't I have learned even more from her? Would I not accept from her, things that would benefit me? Once again, I made up my mind to put judgment aside, at least for a few minutes, and to learn from Shari.

This was my next half-question/half-statement: I feel that what sets you apart, Shari, is your ability to talk at eye-level.

In my mind, yes, absolutely. But in my actions, ... I am not always as successful. My humanity and my level of care for others are embedded in my essence. However, in order to remain at "eye-level" all of the time, it is necessary to also be vulnerable and keep an open heart.

Not that I wasn't at eye-level before, but I also had a lot of vulnerability, anger. I was unprepared to cope with various situations. But, with much work, I managed to narrow that by a greater and greater extent. Today, if I see someone who is suffering, is acting improperly, or is angry, and takes it out on me, or on others within their environment, it is much easier for me to maintain a state of grace and compassion. I try not to take it personally.

Still, I do experience some difficulty with this, and I aspire to narrow the gap in their frequency. There are positive frequencies, such as love and happiness that uplift you, and negative frequencies, such as anger and disappointment that bring you down.

And, many times, I continue to be aware that there are certain frequencies that bring me down and close my heart as a form of self-defense. I am still working on this, still trying to keep my own frequency constantly high and empowered, and my heart open, no matter what frequency enters my space. That is the only way you can positively influence your surroundings.

I thought about how hard it was not to be influenced by those belittling and critical frequencies, and not just the ones coming from the outside, but those that came from inside too. How many times have I had a distinct inner feeling tell me what I should do, but I did not know if that feeling was genuine, or if I was merely interpreting it that way. In other words, I did not know what people would say about me if I did what I wanted to do; how it would influence me, or if I would even be successful.

When I begin to think, the fears rise in me and I stop to wait for something to happen to make it clear to me what is the right thing to do. But once I begin doing that, I am no longer listening in a pure way because I have allowed the fear to rise—the fear of not being successful, or of making mistakes. The fear of being hurt constantly whispers in my ear, telling me that unless I know with certainty the right thing to do, I had better not even try it. That had been my pattern of behavior until the guides of "The Council of Six" presented me with an entirely different approach to the concept of making a mistake.

"In our terms, there is no such thing as a 'mistake.' The concept of a mistake, as it exists in the Western world, does not match our perception of it.

"You have come into the world to gain experience and to learn from your experiences. Some of your experiences are supposed to make things difficult for you, make you fail, take you down unexpected paths, and lead you to unexpected thoughts. If you had taken only the safe and tried way, you would never have learned. The more possibilities that are presented, the more possible turns and crossroads there will be that will allow you to make decisions, and the more opportunities you will have to gain experience and learn.'

"But today, in your world, people have stopped allowing room for the way to be taken and allow room only for the outcome. As far as we here in the beyond are concerned, the outcome is often meaningless. When you act in a way that is not good for you, all you have to do is change the way taken.

"When you regard something as a mistake, you immediately stop. You are triggering feelings that have nothing to do with the issue at hand—guilt, fear, pain, frustration. These feelings create in you a sense of danger that prevents you from acting the same way again. This also goes against what we believe in, because it is often the difference between the first time you took a certain path and the second time you took it that causes you to learn something new. The circumstances have changed, and, therefore, the second time, you might well be successful. Many of you stop immediately after the first time and call it a mistake. There are many examples in your world of people who have tried things over and over until they succeed.

"We would like to remind you that there is no such thing as making a mistake—only gaining an experience. Many times, you consider something to be a mistake, and in retrospect it is ultimately revealed to be something positive. At other times, something you at first considered to be good, in retrospect, is discovered to be bad. Do not judge the way in terms of right or wrong. Such terms do not exist in reality. There is a "right-for-you-at-this-current-moment." that is a fundamental difference. The concept of right and wrong describes a situation in which there is only one way possible, as if there is just one thing that is right for you, and is crucial. The other possibility presents you with a colorful path having countless variations and possibilities with endless turns to select. And yes, some will ultimately lead in a not-suitable direction, and that is all.

"Should you be willing to go down this different path, and realize that, to a certain extent, every path is always somewhat like a maze in which you sometimes hit a wall and need to turn, you will eventually get the result you seek. It is an entirely different approach.

"We suggest you remove the word 'mistake' from your dictionaries and replace it with the word 'experience.' Sometimes, an experience that does not work for you may be just the right thing for another person. If you can realize that there is no single truth—that a so-called mistake is considered to be a mistake only in your own judgement (not the judgement of others), you will be able to free yourselves of much fear and many inhibitions.

"So, our blessing to you is that you should make many mistakes, as you call them, because you learn the most from your mistakes. Actually, you should allow yourselves to experience many things, because that is why you are here in this incarnation, and we will accompany you always."

I try to remember the guides' words, recognizing that I have so often done things I considered to be mistakes only to discover eventually that those very mistakes worked to my advantage.

Honestly, there are still times when I am afraid to make a mistake. Shari chimed in, saying:

I, too, have always been aware that there are no mistakes; that there are only experiences. Even when something looked like a mistake, I felt that it was part of a learning experience for me. I felt that I had grown and been nurtured by it.

Do You Know How to Recognize Your Feelings?

It seemed to me that Shari had found a way of her own to overcome fear; to keep listening to her inner voice despite the "noise" or that fear within us all. I wondered if she simply ignored these feelings, or coped with them in a different way than the way I did.

First, you need to familiarize yourself with the complete spectrum of feelings and emotions: love, happiness, excitement, wonder, curiosity and innovativeness, anger, insult, hurt, narrow-mindedness, belittlement, pain, anxiety, and jealousy.

But, what does "familiarize yourself with the complete spectrum" mean?

Getting to know those feelings inside yourself. In the same way I experience them. Not to simply know in the abstract that they exist. If anger flares in me, how does it feel? What does it look like to me? What shade or color does it have? What intensity? You need to study these feelings, just as if you are doing research for a thesis about yourself and your feelings. You need to experience them firsthand, to allow them.

Most people turn "outside" when they are angry. I am angry because you did this or that to me. There is blame. Guilt then quickly follows because a voice was raised perhaps, or someone was too insulting. Instead of going through that kind of drama, you could simply sit quietly and feel—allow yourself to feel.

When I do that, the first thing I feel is that my body is cringing and resisting. We do not really want to feel. We may say I'm angry, or I'm afraid, but we do not allow this feeling to rise in us completely so that we can observe it. For a long time I was afraid to feel. (And I felt a lot!) I did not understand how afraid I was. It is interesting, this contradiction—being a person who feels a lot yet still follows a pattern that demonstrates a fear of feeling.

I know all about that, I said, and we both laughed in empathy with each other.

So, it's important to allow one's feelings to exist, to be, so that we can become familiar with their complete spectrum; to release our judgment about feelings—because there is a lot of judgment involved.

What do you mean by "judgment?"

People often talk about positive feelings and negative feelings. There are feelings that you are permitted to experience, such as happiness and security; then there are feelings that it is suggested you stop, like sadness, fear, and shame.

Yes, I agreed silently. Many times, when certain feelings had arisen in me, I wondered whether it was alright to feel them. For example, when I am insulted or hurt by someone, there is a voice in me that asks, what's there to be insulted about? It is a familiar voice, one that originated at home and comes from my childhood.

As children, we were taught that when something was hurting, we were to overcome the pain. Because, what else can you do? Today, I understand that overcoming pain is wonderful, but we must first allow ourselves to feel that pain.

I tried then to make unpleasant feelings go away quickly. In fact, I don't allow myself, or, to be more accurate, I didn't allow myself in the past, to take the time to experience unpleasant feelings.

But, it wasn't only unpleasant feelings that I prevented myself from experiencing. I used to do the same with feelings of strength, of success, of love given by those around me. All of those frightened me. What if they weren't real, I used to think? Maybe if I were to let myself feel successful I would actually appear arrogant and condescending? Or, maybe this will go away soon and I will feel pain instead?

I have had many reasons to avoid feelings; to judge feelings in terms of those that are "allowed," and those that are "forbidden." Was that what Shari meant?

What do you mean by "allow yourself to feel?"

When a feeling rises within, it is necessary first to identify it correctly. Many times we are subjected to a turbulence of feelings, but we fail to understand what it is we are actually feeling. If we sit quietly for a moment, and allow the body to speak—perhaps even to ask ourselves, what am I feeling right now—then all of the feelings will begin to surface; sadness, anger, frustration, helplessness, guilt, blame. This might take the form of one feeling, or two, or maybe all feelings. You simply need to give room to each one of them.

The moment I acknowledge that I feel X, and I allow myself to feel Y, the turbulence simply fades away. It is like magic.

Allowing a feeling is not about saying I'm sad, it's about feeling the sadness; letting the sadness come forward and to actually say to myself that I am allowing myself to feel the sadness. At the same time, I reject that sadness. I do not want to be sad. The moment I recognize that I do not want to be sad, the two things collide.

The sadness tries to rise up, but I don't want to be sad, so I'm stuck. But, if I allow myself to feel the sadness, recognize that I'm sad, and acknowledge that I also wish to reject that sadness, it fades. It may happen in this moment of recognition that I will be subjected to many feelings—I need to name each and every one of them.

Actually, I can feel both sadness and happiness at the same time.

Of course. And I think that the moment you recognize your feelings more, and give them room, you also make room for more happiness. Then you can truly feel both sadness and happiness at the same time, because you recognize that it is like an energy that rises and dissipates.

And what stops us from feeling that is the fear of experiencing it?

There are various levels of "not feeling." There are those who build an inner wall, who suffer from an inner blindness and do not want to know, or they do not want to feel and deal with it. Period. That is one level.

Then there is a level at which we do feel, but we are being so judgmental toward ourselves that we attempt to push the feeling inside. We push and push until it can't be pushed any more. What happens then? The feeling transforms into a kind of volcano inside the body. It erupts. It erupts in the form of anger and aggression.

However, if you simply allow it—like opening a pressure cooker, letting the steam, the energy, to be released safely—then there is no reason for an outburst. There is no judgment at all in God, the essence of things.

We are spirits who have come here to experience. It is not for nothing that we possess an entire spectrum of feelings. But we, as human beings, divide these feelings into good and bad. Thus, we need to be familiar with the complete spectrum of feelings; so we can choose. I am familiar with sadness, but I wish to be happy.

So long as I understand that there are waves; that I do not push a feeling down. If I do not judge the sadness, I can easily transform it. I can let it rise. I can feel. I can respect that feeling and then change it for something else.

I felt I needed a moment to process Shari's words. On the one hand, I knew from my own experience, that if you allow a feeling to rise, it could change into another feeling. I also know that no feeling remains constant forever. Even when you are sad, you might still experience moments of happiness. And, in times of happiness, moments of sadness may be mixed in.

Each time I allowed myself to let a feeling rise, it always passed after a time. On the other hand, Shari spoke about helping the feeling pass. That if I dared to feel it, and understand what I was feeling, I would be able to actively transform it; change it to another feeling.

I realized that I had done that in the past unintentionally. Sometimes when I had been sad I thought about something good, and the feeling changed, but that phenomenon only occurred when I had allowed myself to feel the sadness.

Many times, I have been afraid to feel, worried that it might prove to be too difficult. The truth, which I now understand, was that I was also afraid to feel powerful and positive feelings. Oh, that fear. . . . !

"Does the fear come from the ego?"

Look, we have our ego, and we have our essence. My essence, as I know it to be, is something very delicate, very quiet, and very harmonious. It is loving, happy, and pure. Any voice within me that is not like that is a part of the ego. The voice of the ego does not come from within the essence.

This does not mean that we should negate the ego. It is an instrument we need, enabling us to learn more about ourselves. But we need to decide, to discern, from which place we are acting, because if I am hurt by someone and I immediately react by defending myself, or by attacking, then my ego is the element in me that is working. But, if I am hurt and I observe this hurt, I know that my reaction to it may be a part of the ego. I see that there is vulnerability in me—which is fine—for there are reasons that I am vulnerable.

Perhaps it stems from my childhood, or perhaps it was acquired in other incarnations. Whatever it is, I observe it, I embrace the feeling, transform it, and I release it. I am then able to choose to reply from a much more accommodating and understanding place.

This does not mean that I shouldn't draw the line, of course, but it does mean that I do not become defensive or aggressive. I draw a line and I conduct myself from a place that is understanding, loving, and caring in a very practical, pure way.

What scared or still scares you?

For many years I had a fear of strength, and therefore possessed a sort of mechanism that belittled myself. Even when people on the outside saw me as great and powerful, I still felt like a frightened little girl inside, no matter what was taking place on the outside. It was a very wide gap, and one that was very difficult to live with.

Slowly, I narrowed this gap down to the very verge of closure. One small step at a time; to intensify my inner strength, to acknowledge my own power, to embrace that place of belittlement, to understand the place that demeans itself, and to release the little girl—she, who is not the one who leads. Make her grow inside me. And, finally, to reach a place at which my inner maturity is the same as my external maturity.

There was a reason why that mechanism was there, inside me. We see the here-and-now, but we have a history of reincarnation, both as individuals and as humanity as a whole.

In that history of reincarnation, both the personal and the collective, I believe that we have inflicted a lot of damage because of power. That power that was not positive, but destructive. I think we have come to Earth to bring change, to bring the light, to be the beacon of a better world—and I view myself as a beacon of light.

We had to have a mechanism that would keep us small while enlarging our inner strength by having a sort of inner promise to grow our values; to not harm others, not be destructive, to instead be a power of light. This can only be done in an aware process of growth, step by step, even as we release the difficult places within us, the places from which anger rises, destructiveness rises, and the will for revenge, hurt, and blame rises. And, while releasing those, it is important to enlarge the power within the light, which is a soothing and soft light that brings about possibilities.

In thinking about Shari, I once again felt the differences between us. Once more, I felt my inner judgment rising. In her experience, it was less difficult to cope with feelings because she has enjoyed proven success, a process that is very empowering. Or, is it actually the other way around?

I think that with you, I said after some thought, that the gap was even more significant than it is with most of us. Outwardly, you have gained proof in the form of business success. I can try to tell myself that, when I come to experience great success, the gap will then be narrowed. But, what you are saying is that the gap does not narrow because of something external.

Right! The gap is an inner one. It is between where we presently are in our lives and where our inner child is. You might be sixty, but still, what drives you is a five-year-old girl. I think the ego problems in the world stem from exactly that place.

You can sometimes look at a meeting of a board of directors and observe that it is like an argument among a group of five-year-olds. Here are people who are very talented, very developed, professional, learned lawyers and professors and economists, but inside, what drives them, are their five-year-old selves carrying a wounded ego—and they are raging. Because I recognized this, both in myself and in others, I took steps to bridge the gap inside, within me, and learned to approach others with compassion.

Whenever I encounter someone acting in an inappropriate way, or in a way that is aligned only with his external aspect, I know that he is being driven by his inner child.

Looking inside myself and in looking around me, I truly can see that there is a gap between the internal and the external that exists in everyone I know. So, as far as you are concerned, among the lessons human beings have to learn is how to narrow this gap?

Yes, but not everyone recognizes this gap inside themselves. There is a lot of self-righteousness, because, when the five-year-old child emerges in the person, they are immediately offended and become defensive and aggressive. Instead of responding, wow, I'm really behaving like a five-year-old now, proving that there is a gap between my standing and my reaction, we look outside ourselves. This is something only we, on our own, can take care of and heal within ourselves.

I thought about how challenging it is to recognize and acknowledge this gap in real time. Although, even if we recognize in retrospect that there is a gap between our behavior and how we would have preferred to behave, we can still seek to understand where the gap is and how we want to change the situation.

For most of my life, I have tried to adapt myself to an inner image I thought would be right for me. For example, I really love to express myself freely, even if it means I will stand out, but I was taught that standing out is dangerous, because it may arouse jealousy or attract objections. And so, every time I did stand out, I panicked, and I took a step back.

The need to do this is powerful, which meant that it happened again and again. It was a painful and frustrating mechanism that did not allow me to be at my best nor to act freely. I think there were gaps in Shari too.

I was interested to learn how she had acted, how she had recognized and changed her internal gap.

For most of my life, I felt that people did not really know me—that I was neither truly seen nor heard.

Today, I look at this in a completely different way. If someone does not see me, that is their choice to make. I already know who I am, and I show the world who I am—a very transparent person—for good, or for bad. One can immediately see on my face whether I am happy or sad; pleased or displeased. What is inside is also on the outside. And anyone who does not see this, simply doesn't see it.

Shari shrugged.

It has been a long process. I have always felt a gap and frustration, but I didn't know what exactly was frustrating me. With a lot of work, I began to see the gaps.

First, to see the little one within, to see the child—then, to see the places inside me as opposed to what I want, seeing, instead, the reflection I got from the external world, that was not what I expected to be getting. There was a huge gap. I felt that I wasn't being seen; that I wasn't being understood—I felt I was relaying a message, and that it was coming in upside-down.

I have done a lot of work involving both internal and external communication, and I have learned to recognize and accept the gap, as well as having managed to change my inner set of concepts. I transformed the gap into a bridge. Wherever I saw a gap, I saw an opportunity for a bridge, and I turned that gap into a bridge. It is an example of the way change is always possible.

As long as I grow, everything continues to change. After all, we are in constant, perpetual motion—we all grow all the time. There are people who do not acknowledge such change; people who say that human beings never change—I will never change. She will never change. There are others who simply do not want to change.

But we undergo change simply by being human; from fetus, to baby, to childhood, to youth, and on into adulthood. We change into mothers and fathers, and become pupils, teachers, and employees, before we grow old, and die.

The very essence of our existence involves continuous change. The moment we acknowledge this, and cherish it, we can also take charge and "lead" the change we want, rather than to simply change through the inertia by which force you are born, live, and die.

Once again, my thoughts traveled back to me and the people I have worked with.

To what extent do we allow ourselves to change? To what extent do we allow ourselves to become familiar with the many aspects of our being? Do we let ourselves become familiar with all of the pieces that compose who we are? I am not necessarily speaking about aspects or sides of us that we do not like, or we believe require improvement.

I find that many people do not dare to connect with the powerful aspects of themselves, nor admit to themselves that they are successful. Often, we wait for others to tell us how wonderful we are. But when we are told, even then we often dismiss it.

I was familiar with both aspects.

I have many times had the feeling that what people see is only what I have allowed them to see; and that there are parts of me that, if I allowed them to be seen, would cause others to avoid my company. I was afraid that there is something inside me that is very difficult for others to contain—a kind of demon or monster that I somehow managed to hide well.

If anyone were to see these other aspects, they would not only be disappointed with me, but would perhaps not even want to be in my company. I have shed many tears because of this feeling.

The most surprising thing for me to discover was that many whom I have led in meetings or workshops have felt exactly the same way. It is as if there was a bubble surrounding us, obscuring our real selves. And God help us should that bubble burst and expose us! We would experience rejection and criticism.

It is sad that so many people think this way, while, in reality, this isn't the case at all. It is one of the most flawed and self-harming things we continue to inflict upon ourselves. It is clear to me that we see this on every level. Consider the people around you. You know aspects of many of them that you have probably never spoken to them about. We feel each other's frequencies—and those frequencies communicate everything!

That said, we see the greatness in a person, even though they may not yet be ready to see it within themselves. Many times we consider a given person to be someone who is not living up to their potential. We feel there is much more in them, even though they, themselves, do not recognize this.

From what does this stem, this fear of ours; the fear of being great, talented, or wonderful? Why do we find this so intimidating?

How Do You Connect Body, Spirit, and Soul?

The meetings I had with Shari were held in her office, the two of us sitting on a sofa. In the moments just before, and as the meeting began, I always felt the connection between us. I can't really explain it (although, believe me, I have tried), but it has always been there. Shari felt it too. It was a sense of intimacy and sisterhood. During such moments, there were no differences or gaps between us, just a sense of togetherness, an all-embracing feeling that I cherished and enjoyed.

At each meeting, after a brief chat during which we talked about the goings on during the past week, I would ask Shari the questions that had blossomed in my mind in the wake of our last meeting. I would ask for clarification about things, ideas, and concepts that I had not fully understood, to make sure I had grasped the full meaning of her words.

With every meeting, I felt how I was changing. In my day-to-day activities, when I was faced with a dilemma, or when I felt some kind of fear, Shari's words would suddenly jump into my head. They opened new opportunities for me, and I was quick to make use of them. I felt a great thirst to hear from Shari, to understand the attitude to life that had contributed to her success.

Looking at yourself today, looking back on the path you have taken, what makes you happiest?

What makes me the happiest is that today I feel that I am one with the Creator; that I am going hand-in-hand with him. I feel that he is with me; that he is within me. It makes me happy that I've managed to clean away all of the internal "dirt"— the shells, the noises, and the karmas. I feel that I have made room to amplify the divine spark inside me, the Creator.

Listening to Shari speak with such passion, directly from her heart, caused me to feel a pang of jealousy. Her words sounded as if they came from such a peaceful, comfortable place. I wanted to feel like that too!

At that point, the same old suspicious feelings flared in me, even as they mixed with an element of cynicism. What did it mean to be "one with the Creator?" How does anyone feel that? While I often feel that connection, I am simultaneously left with many questions and doubts. Was this what Shari meant? I had a feeling that it wasn't, not really. Perhaps, when I am left with doubt, I am missing something?

What does it feel like, being one with the Creator? I asked her.

"It feels like I am protected, guarded, loved and beloved. That doesn't mean I don't have a human side. Don't be confused. I sometimes feel vulnerable and experience insecurity, but these days I know how to be a soul inside a body—not two separate things, but a single whole.

During one of my channelings, one I wrote about years ago for "Essence of Life," I was given a set of twenty-two values. One of them was that we are, all of us, both souls and human beings. There are people who do not believe in anything about the beyond and there are people who believe that they are souls who have entered the experience of a human being.

I've been through an interesting process in that regard. I have always been able to feel my soul. But now, today, I understand that one must give room to the actuality that, inside the body, within the physical body, there exists also the human aspect that reflects all our feelings and all our sensations, whether they are emotional, physical, or mental.

The whole human aspect of things is there; the dense matter—because a human being is matter as well as spirit. We also possess the spiritual; the divine spark, our souls—and the process of ascension involves integrating the two. In that process of integration there is a connection with the Creator, with creation. And there, within that integration, everything is light, love, acceptance, unity, and serenity. It is the light. It exists inside of me alongside the human aspect. Therefore, there is a process of integration and choice. It is a matter of choosing which aspect is leading the way.

So then, being connected to God is about allowing your soul to lead the way?

Yes.

And, for example, when I am in doubt I am returning the control to the human aspect?

Exactly.

But people get confused about the human aspect. That is because we have a side of humanity that allows us to love, to be compassionate, and to be giving. It is this, set alongside the primal, animalistic side of us, that reacts.

When someone is in doubt, it is the human, reactive aspect of that person that is being dominant. That is not a bad thing, necessarily. There is no good and bad in this.

We, our souls, have come here to experience life in the material; inside a human. It is part of the process. There is an experience here, and a way to achieve ascension; a way to become one with the light.

So, the ascension is about remaining as attentive as possible to the soul, and as little as possible to the rest? To allow our feelings to come to the surface and stop the reactive, automatic mechanism?

It is about being attentive to everything. All the voices. It is to allow each and every voice its room, but to always choose the spiritual voice, the light.

And what happens when we are drawn by human thoughts?

That happens to all of us. Sometimes we fall into a sort of pit, but we need to learn to accept even that as well, because it is a part of the path we need to take.

We are talking about spirituality, about remembrance. So, when I say today that I am connected with the Creator, I keep reminding myself that it is by my choice. My choice is to be in the light. My choice is to be connected with my soul.

And, should I happen to fall, then I simply fall. I have the opportunity to experience another purification, another ascension, one more cleansing process; more work to do. I accept that—not always with pleasure, but definitely with love.

I have had hope so many times that the developmental work I was doing would bring me to a place where there was no more dilemma, no more indecision, and no more challenging conflict. I thought that, if the right guides existed out there, the moment I connected with them they would take charge of and be responsible for my life. They would direct me down a safe path, one on which no mistakes would ever occur, and I would never be hurt nor ever experience uncomfortable situations.

With time, and after connecting with several guides, I realized that such a specific kind of guide does not exist, because the purpose of our essence here in this world has to do with our experiencing and learning.

I am aware that the path I took has certainly helped me to cope with challenge in multiple ways, having less drama and providing more results. Still, I had to ask Shari about it. Perhaps she had, or knew of, some trick or shortcut that I was not aware of.

And does that mean that now everything will be easy in life? Shari laughed.

No. Definitely not, but it does mean that I now feel loved. I feel protected. I feel I now possess an inner knowledge that everything that comes to me is always to my advantage, regardless of whether my interpretation of it is positive or negative. It comes to teach me, to offer me self-precision, and, while directing me to the right place, it pushes me to take action.

Sometimes we suffer blows that make us stop and think. Wait! Why? Why do I deserve this? What have I done?

It is important to understand that whatever it is, it has come to push you into making progress. That does not mean that life will become easy, but by following those precepts, I was able to accept life more and more as it was, even if it were to hold things that are very difficult and complicated.

Shari's words made me think about the many fairytales that end, "and they lived happily ever after."

Wasn't that what I longed for? Isn't that what we all long for? For something to happen, and, from that moment on, our lives would become easy and simple? That we would one day develop enough to feel that we have reached our destination and can rest?

One of the clearest things that the guides of the Council of Six repeated over and over is that the physical world is a place of doing and learning. Doing and learning are the primary reasons we have come here to earth. To gain experiences, to learn, and to develop.

The guides say that what makes it difficult for most humans is judgment.

When we define something as difficult, or as unfair, it is difficult for us to cope with this. It would be much easier for us if we viewed that something as a milestone we need to pass.

Joy, the council guide who always chooses to bring happiness and laughter, says that describing life as a "journey," makes us see things that get in our way to be more difficult and burdensome, because that is the common meaning of the word "journey." She suggests instead that we view life as a "trip." Trips can also be difficult. You can experience heat, rain, mud, exhaustion, and many other unhappy events. Even so, most of us do not view a trip as a burden, even if it presents difficulty.

On the contrary, people often seek to go on a challenging trip. And what if life is a challenging trip, one that sometimes contains genuinely difficult elements we could have done without? Don't we, on occasion, look back and take great satisfaction from thinking about a crisis we have surpassed, meeting a challenge we have overcome?

I thought that Shari was suggesting that we stop expecting everything to be easy, and realize that life brings us many possibilities—some good, some challenging.

Still, though, something in me refused to let go.

So, does this mean that when you have reached this place, you can rest?

"Doing" is creation, and as I have already said, creation never ceases. In creation, there is constant perpetual movement, death and birth, and growth and flourishing.

We are like nature. If we accept the natural motion and flow of things, then we are peaceful, because we know it is simply the process. Like waves, coming and going; like the ebb and flow of the tide. We move that way as well, even when we may be unaware of it. If we do not resist it, but accept it instead, as a part of our nature and of creation, we achieve much inner peace.

The "doing" continues, as well as there is growth.

There is still much work to do, and new ideas to explore, all of the time, in many and diverse areas. There is the sense that this is a circle; that there is something that connects it all.

Today, all this is done from a completely different place—from within a place of inner peace.

This inner peace, isn't it created because you are no longer criticized, not because everything has fallen into place?

No. The external things are still there. I am still being criticized, but the inner peace is unrelated to the external things. It is created from the inner connection.

Inner peace is created from being connected inwardly?

Yes, finding the inner connection is a years-long process that has brought me to purer beliefs, purer behavioral patterns and habits, knowing how and when to release this or that person from my life, knowing how and when to release concepts; to release and transform feelings, step-by-step-by-step, with much introspection and inner work.

In this book you talk about how you have taken these many steps during the whole of your life. You speak of how, at every step, you stopped to check: Who am I? What am I? Where am I?

Where does the gap exist between the "me" that I want to be and the "who" that I am now? You then chose what you wanted. And, after making yourself more precise, you ascended to the next level. That's the ascension process, isn't it?"

Perhaps it is more precise that I describe it as a spiral—a spiral that starts from the bottom and continues rising all the time; even moving as a circle. When you come to a given step's end and close the circle of that step, you are already now at a higher place. You keep rising, going up and up, in a circular motion, a step at a time. That is how we develop.

We often say to ourselves, "Ugh! Do I really need to go through this again? Why is this happening to me again?"

Things do not really repeat themselves, because each time the insights and observations are different; the viewpoint is different, so you cope with it differently.

It is very important to see this as development, because many times we fall, and we say to ourselves, "I thought I had come so far. I thought I had made so much progress. Now here I am. I'm back at the starting point!"

But you do not actually go back. True, you might be learning something you had supposedly already learned, but you are still making progress and moving on. You will already be in a different place. That is important to note.

The "doing" develops and changes in the same way you develop and change—each time from a different place—both from a different internal place and a different external place—because everything is a reflection.

That reminds me of school, of when we learned math in first, grade, math in third grade and math in fourth grade.

Exactly. When you are in college, you study advanced mathematics from a completely different place. We keep learning, always from different places. We keep advancing and moving forward. We take steps in personal development, but because we are dealing with issues that feel like they are identical, we feel like we are stuck or even going backward. But we constantly keep progressing.

School, the progression of the classes we take and the stages involved, is an excellent and precise metaphor. If we take this metaphor even further, it is important to realize that in personal development there are teachers, methods, and various ways of learning that are individually suited.

One teacher would be suitable for the first grade, another for the twelfth, and a third for college. Knowledge pertaining to personal development also has stages and requires teacher-suitability, each teacher suitable for a different step, or a path that is suitable for each stage. And just as in school, I can love a certain teacher, while another child will find that teacher hard to get along with. It's very much about who is most suitable for you at each specific stage, and who is personally suitable for you .

A first-grade teacher can't simply walk into a high school classroom and begin teaching.

No, because it requires a different set of skills which they don't have. It is the same with spiritual teachers. Each one adjusts to what is most fitting for them to teach or to learn.

I know that when we first spoke about this, my perception was hurtful to you, bothered you. It wasn't easy for you to accept my saying that one teacher might be better for a particular student than another teacher—that there are different teachers and different paths for each level.

I think that many times, in personal and spiritual development, teachers speak in a language that uses a set of definitions that might sound very offensive to students. When they speak about "high frequencies" and "low frequencies," for example, those terms might be misinterpreted as condescending or judgmental.

Such interpretations cause damage and separation instead of the understanding that there are a great number of frequencies—it is like a building with a hundred floors. You have the first, the second, the third, and on to the hundredth floor. No one can say that one floor is right and another isn't.

There are frequencies that are more dense, are closer to the ground, and there are frequencies that are airier, more open—different. These are higher frequencies, ones closer to the hundredth floor. No one of them is "good" or "bad."

As Shari spoke, I could feel the resistance hardening in me. Obviously, we each learn and advance, but my learning happens in comparison to myself, not by looking at others. What I mean to say is that it isn't right to judge one learning, one personal or spiritual development, as having more worth than another. They come into expression in different ways with different people, but that does not make one good or the other bad. When it is said that one person is in first grade and another is in college, there may be the feeling that the latter is in a better place than the former; that the first floor isn't as good as the hundredth.

But even when you speak about it, Shari, I feel resistance building up in me because I naturally assume that the hundredth floor must be better than the first.

Why?

I don't know. Maybe because an apartment on the hundredth floor is more expensive than an apartment on the first floor? I smiled.

But that doesn't make it good or not good, it is only a question of height. In channeling, for example, there is more light as you ascend, more love and pleasantness; there is a different frequency, a different density of frequency than that on the earth's surface.

Right.

No one is ever angry at someone for being in the first grade instead of the fourth grade.

But someone in the fourth grade is more developed than someone who is in the first grade. So, when you tell someone that you are in the fourth grade and remark that they are still only in the first. . . .

That is true, but that is simply the way things are. What you are describing are the developmental stages. You are more advanced today than you were before.

Very true. But, still, you cannot compare one person's development to another's.

The development, the introspection, one's climbing up and ascending the various steps and stages, these all become easier the farther you go on your path. The beginning is slow and difficult. It begins with survival and soul-searching, only then do you begin to shed layers, beginning with the ones you don't want. Then you move on to the ones you want to keep, as you continue to shed more and more layers.

I think that as long as I have the "human" in me, there won't be a time when I will have no layers at all.

There are many times when I have protected myself from something by resisting it with a "shell," as you call it. And even when I removed it, I discovered that there was yet another shell beneath it, and then another. Do you feel there are still more shells in you?

I feel I have reached some sort of core.

There are no more shells, I asked Shari? I was surprised to hear this. I had assumed that shedding was an endless process.

Yes. I feel I have reached the core; of the human aspect too. Not that the human aspect is gone. It's just that it has no more layers. At present, I see it as a "completed package."

There is the human place inside me, and there is the light, and there is God inside me. The process I undergo today involves the integration and shifting of weight from the human to the spiritual, from the condensed to the light. That is the place I am at right now.

I have dealt for many years with the removal of the layers, and I spoke about it at length in my first book, Birth: When the Spiritual and the Material Come Together. Today, I feel that what is leading me is the light inside me. It is leading to the integration of both of the cores into one—which is actually the light.

That is encouraging. It means that the process is worthwhile. That it is, after all, finite.

There is no finiteness to the universe and no finiteness to creation. There is no such thing as finite.

There is, however, a perpetual change of form and there is constant development, growth and evolution, and development and movement. All of the time. But it is different from the hard and frustrating work that is the removal of the difficulties; removing the shells, the survival, the fear. It becomes a different process. And it isn't like you ever reach some sort of end.

So, the optimism lies in the fact that there will come a time, eventually, when you can look at yourself and see everything. No more shells. It doesn't mean that you will no longer be afraid of anything, but that there is transparency.

Exactly!

I thought about how I was actually there. I was actually quite in the throes of this process. I found that the more layers I shed, the more I discovered still others I felt I ought, too, to release.

I tried to think about how it was that I had started, and I could not remember. I assumed that this was a part of my development I was simply not aware of. I thought, perhaps, that I could turn it into a conscious process—pay attention to the layers I had. It should then become easier for me to understand and to choose which of them I wanted to release, which was actually what Shari had suggested I do. It seemed like an endless process of release and growth, and I asked Shari how to begin.

You begin with what you don't want and follow that with what you do want.

Interesting.

That was what my process was like at least. Again, I don't think there is a single or precise recipe for everyone. Even when you learn spiritualism and self-development, or get it from this book and the insights that I advocate, it is possible that you will find that one thing will be suitable for you, and you will embrace it, and something else will be less suitable; this is perfectly fine. There is no single way or measure that fits all.

For me, it was very clear. First, I realized what I did not want. At that time I noticed that there was a lot of aggression around me. It appeared in the words and body language. I realized that I did not want that violence in my life. There was a lot of extroverted behavior in my life, too; many parties, many events, and much traveling.

While I still attend parties and events, I have come to realize that what is more important to me has to do with substance—meaningful conversations, personal development, connecting with people who are on the same frequency as I am, people who speak my language, and being with people with whom I feel understood.

There has been much misunderstanding in my life. People misunderstood me, laughed at me, mocked me; they said I was crazy. I felt I had to constantly justify myself and be someone other than myself. This caused me to feel much of the time that something wasn't right with me—that I was different.

I gradually realized that those people and their behavioral patterns were not right for me; that such situations did not work for me. Even some of what were supposed to be life's pleasures didn't really feel right. It took me a long time to understand that. It sounds simple, but it's not. I had to redefine everything anew.

In my soul there is love for all humanity. I have an elevated point of view that we are all one, all connected, and that we have all come from God and will one day return to God.

I had to learn all of that inside of this body, inside Shari's body. I had to find what is right for me, what is fitting for me. I had to find in my day-to-day what makes me feel good and what doesn't.

The moment I knew what it was that I *didn't* want, I had to start peeling those layers away within myself.

If those things had gotten into my life, it must have been something inside me that magnetized them; attracted them. It wasn't something external. It was, without question, internal.

What do you mean by magnetized?

It is the power of attraction that brings things to you and "glues" them to you, like metal to a magnet. It is the same thing with people and situations in our lives. There are those who suffer from a shortage of money, so they regularly magnetize situations that create such shortages of money.

Or, it could be a shortage of love. Such a person might be very rich, and, while they feel they have plenty in the materialistic aspect, they feel lacking in love. They will magnetize to their lives situations that demonstrate to them that there is no love.

If there are situations or people in our life that we do not love, but who come back into it over and over, I recommend that you look inside to check which thought, which belief, which emotion, has magnetized, has drawn, that person or situation to your life. It can be fear, it can take the form of a belief, it might be a childhood memory, or, perhaps, karma from previous incarnations. They are the internal things that cause the external things.

So, this never simply happens for no reason?

In my opinion, no. There is a reason for everything. I think it is part of a plan we bring with us as souls. Put into other words, if I have come here to experience something, I will continue to encounter it until I have learned my lesson. I have to get inside it every time, deeper and deeper, to release fears, release patterns, release restrictive beliefs, release any feeling, emotion, belief or thought that prevents me from achieving the result I want. And that is a process.

Shari's words supported the messages I had been receiving from my spiritual guides. The magnetizing always hap-

pens. We magnetize according to who we are at a particular point in time. For example, if I am preoccupied with my fears, I will not be able to magnetize abundance or a good relationship.

The guides of the Council of Six explain that we must create an internal reality, a good feeling that we identify with, so we will be able to create a change in reality.

For many years, I attached no importance to this. I had been taught that, in order to change, one simply had to do things. But that often failed to work for me. I was unable to change things, and I could not understand why. The words of the guides helped me to understand that as long as I did not feel successful on the inside, I could never experience success on the outside.

We are taught that the things that happen to us in life shape who we are. Sometimes that is true, especially when significant things happen, but, in the day-to-day of the things that occupy us, it is the other way around. First, we need to see the thing happening and feel ourselves becoming different. Only then will the change happen in reality—and only if we believe that such a change is possible.

So, the first stage requires the realization that change is possible.

There are things within our personal control that can be changed; attitudes and patterns, the echoing, the energy that might present a different situation, the thoughts, the choices, and how we conduct ourselves. There are also things that require a collective change. Until a collective decision is made to create something new out of the old by a critical mass of people who want and resonate the same thing—without that collective will, change simply won't happen.

So, how do you choose what to change?

You take off one layer after another of what it is that magnetizes those people to you, of what magnetizes those situations. Once I began to release more and more, I was also better able to identify what I wanted, what made me feel good, which people I felt most comfortable with, which situations are comfortable for me, and what I enjoy doing. I have learned a lot about myself in that way.

I can now say, as far as I am concerned, that's it. I have reached the core; the essence. I can now, at any particular moment, simply check whether something is suitable for me or it's not; the core operates like a sort of seismograph. Very simple.

Today, when something isn't right for me, I can feel it. There is a tightening in my stomach, a feeling of discomfort, a sense of insult, a feeling that I'm not in the right place. I can find myself in a certain situation and immediately respond: Wait a minute. No! I want to be in a place where I feel good and I am comfortable. And that's it.

When I say "in a place," I mean a place that is primarily internal and only then external.

And how do you define this essence, this core?

Think about a fruit from which you can peel layer after layer until you finally reach the core—an apricot pit, for example. That is the core of a human being. Their essence.

I, too, believe there is a personality core in each of us; a core we came into this world with—a sort of "behavioral DNA." This core contains a few essential traits that accompany us throughout our lives. When we become familiar enough with them to live by them fully, we are able to lead a life that is more loyal to who we really are, and leading such a life brings higher levels of satisfaction and fulfillment.

So, when you reach the core, you can no longer peel away more layers?

There is no need to peel and, indeed, there is nothing left to peel. The core is your essence. How you fulfill your essence in the day-to-day, when you reach the core, well now, that is a different story altogether.

When spiritual people and channelers spoke about 2012 as the year when the end of the world would come, I thought it, instead, would be the end of an era. It would be one age coming to a close, and another world beginning; a new world.

Until that time we would be preparing our "vessels," our bodies, to reach down to the essence. Until that moment we would live in bodies divided by gender—all a mask, all about the layers. Next, we would need to learn to live our essence, our souls, the light, the divine spark— live it in the human body, on the surface of the earth. That is something we have never done as humanity.

Until today, to become light we had to die and leave this dimension, the physical world. The next lesson, the next process or path, involves living the essence, living the God within, living the light on Earth.

Amen.

Amen.

We shared a thoughtful silence. My mind slowly absorbed Shari's words. What a long path she had traveled. Once again, I felt my jealousy of the place she had reached. Shari must have felt it, too, because she smiled at me sympathetically and continued.

These days, I am in a sort of inner spring of water, a place where it is peaceful and comfortable most of the time. But that doesn't mean that tomorrow, or a minute from now, there won't be something else that comes to the surface, like one emerging from water. And I will then have to say to myself, "Oh, this is something that I need to release now," or, "that is something I need to look at now." I'm not fooling myself into thinking that this state will maintain forever.

Some odd feeling could emerge, and I will suddenly be sad without even knowing why. Do I accept this? Do I observe this? Is it something internal? Is it the influence of something external?

It is an ongoing process. I think the acceptance of this ongoing process is what really brings peace. Once, I was very eager to reach the finish line—for most of my life, actually. I wanted to transcend to reach enlightenment, a state of absolute inner peace, but now I know there is no such thing. There is only more. More inner peace, more enlightenment, more tranquility.

So, there is never a finish line, a point after which you can finally rest?

No. This is a marathon that doesn't have a finish. It is ongoing. It is the continuous process of our lives.

I was suddenly overcome by tiredness. I had invested a lot of work in development, in attempts to remove obstacles from my way, to peel away the shells, but the more shells I removed, the more shells I discovered inside. For a single moment, I was exhausted by the effort, especially by the thought that it was never going to end. Perhaps there was no point to this? Why should I bother to strain so hard to listen inwardly? Why should I pay attention to what arose in me, try to understand, to purify, to change, if still more needed work is constantly being discovered?

When you talk about this, it doesn't sound as if you are sad that it is an ongoing process. It doesn't sound as if it tires you."

It doesn't, really. I know now that it is simply what life is; to always be in motion, to always be in development. Things always come up, things always happen. Good and bad are simply the interpretations we put on it. Everything simply happens. The interpretation is ours.

In your books, you talk about the afterlife—so, is it good or is it bad when someone dies? For one man it is the end of the world, while for another it is the realization that he has ascended to a different place. He has changed form and has a whole new life. It's just not in the body he had been occupying. It is only we who interpret this as a bad thing.

I, too, know from the words of the guides that there is no such thing as good or bad, that it is only our judgment. Furthermore, sometimes something that seems good to us at first, turns out down the line to be bad, and sometimes something we believe is bad, we later understand has positively influenced our lives. Good and bad are concepts that stem from our judgmental perspective.

Still, I must admit that, despite my understanding, I often continue to find myself relating to things as being just that, good or bad. However, I felt that Shari was able to be much less judgmental. Shari, how do you do that?

Let's take the weather as an example. It changes all the time. One day is sunny with a clear sky, another day is cloudy, or rainy, drizzling, icy cold, or too hot. These different states are essential to the world, to nature. For me, it's wonderful when it's hot and sunny outside. As far as I am concerned, it is the most pleasant thing there is, but I also know people who think it is the greatest suffering.

I smiled. I mentioned one of my best friends who is always too hot all summer long and simply can't wait for fall to arrive. This caused Shari to smile, too.

As far as those people are concerned, hot weather is horrendous. They feel too hot and uncomfortable. They perspire too much and have little energy.

For me, winter used to be the terrible time with its rain, storms, and cold temperatures. I just couldn't stand it. I remember people around me smiling happily, "What fun, it's raining!" Today, because I am learning to accept the different situations that occur in life. I understand that there are things I enjoy more, and others I enjoy less, but there is nothing that I would call terrible. So, what is good and what is bad?

So, now I also like winters, but, in the past, when I was young and had fun in the swimming pool and at the beach, summer meant the freedom of vacation, and I loved it. I couldn't wait for summer to come. Does that mean summers used to be good then, but today are less so? Maybe it would be more timely to say that today I feel less comfortable about summer than I once did. This does not make summers good, but, equally, it does not make them bad.

I asked Shari, When did you feel you were able to stop viewing things in terms of they being good and bad?

I still look at things that way. On the conscious, cognitive level I understand that things are neither good nor bad, they are simply as they are . . . period. However, on the human, basic, level, if something negative happens to someone who is close to me, it is bad.

I smiled internally with relief. Then I wasn't the only one who viewed things as good or bad. It appeared that that is what we human beings are—simply human.

Time passes from the moment we are able to understand things until we are able to apply them. The impressive thing about Shari is that she refuses to give up. She continues down the path until she reaches her goal. I asked her to elaborate further on the subject of the level of the conscious.

Conscience is the higher perspective, an illuminated observation, one that is beyond my own personal, smaller perspective. It is on the soulful level, the level of the divine plan, the level on which everything is related to everything else, the level on which, even when a disaster happens, you are able to understand that it had a reason.

That's because we learn from it and the world has changed because of it. On the personal level, however, if something thing happens to us or to someone close to us, it is hard for us to accept. It hurts, it frustrates. Those are the moments when you ask God, "Why?"

But that is a very personal level. It is different from the larger, wider picture. I think there are some people who are able to see only at the personal level, and others who see the whole; who see the soulful level, the general level. A look from above. A different sort of view. But this does not mean you no longer retain the human observation, the smaller-scale, private way of looking at things. I think we all have that. We are still human beings; we are both body and soul.

I agreed with her. I believe you cannot be in a state of higher consciousness all the time. We live in the physical world, which forces us to cope with earthly things.

Shari, during the past few months that we have been meeting, I have gained the feeling about you that, even when something difficult happens, you experience it as bad at the first moment, however, you have already gone through very unpleasant things that could have crushed another individual.

To say that I find something bad at first, is misleading. Something can be very saddening, or maddening, but, ultimately, I have the inner knowledge that everything is for the best—that it comes to purify, advance, quicken, fine tune. If I have the inner awareness, then no matter what happens, it will always turn out to be to my advantage. And that is because what has happened is for the sake of evolving. We are constantly evolving, both individually and collectively.

What you say is very beautiful. When something difficult happens to you, no matter the reason, you are there, first of all. You are present and you experience it through to the end. You do not begin to consider why did this happen. You ultimately remember in your conscious mind that everything is to your higher advantage, even if it is difficult to bear in that moment. You do not say that from the beginning, but you first allow yourself to feel.

Absolutely. I entirely feel the pain and feel the frustration.

To me, that is brave.

I have traveled a long and difficult path to get where I am. It is much easier not to cope; to blame, to vent our feelings on someone or something else and say that it is all because of a particular person, because of the country, or because of the general atmosphere. It is much easier to point an accusatory finger at another than to take responsibility, cope, or allow yourself to feel.

But such an attitude will never lead to growth and development, neither on the personal level nor the collective level. So it is necessary to stop and feel and allow these feelings to emerge.

Yes, I do feel injustice. I feel insult. I feel shame. I feel all of those feelings. And then I remember that this has all come to teach me, to teach the environment; to develop, to empower, and to advance. It has come for some reason.

I can give you an example of something that happened to make me ask myself why I needed to cope—and what I needed to do to let go.

When I was fifteen, living in America, I had a boyfriend. He was a Native-American Cherokee whose nickname was "Tomahawk." He had a different real name, very unique, that I haven't heard since those times. Then, recently, while I was watching a television program, someone said that unusual name.

I was not thinking about that boyfriend as I went on watching, but an internal question did, eventually, surface—which karma would I need to release?

When I heard my boyfriend's name, I was shocked. I thought perhaps I had misheard the name. The next day, as I watched the next episode, I saw a man reading a newspaper and Tomahawk's real name was there in the headline. It was then that I realized that I had to go back to age fifteen, observe what I had had with that person, and release it.

Wow! And did you release it? Do you feel that this helped?

We'll wait to see if it helped, but I released a pattern that had been accompanying me. I looked at the relationship I had had then, at age fifteen, and recognized a thread that had woven itself through my entire life.

I asked which karma I had to release, and received a sign. Through that sign I was able to embark on the process of recreating and doing the necessary work. That sort of thing happens to me all the time.

Still, while Shari had been undergoing a process of spiritual development for many years, my first thought was that it did not sound to me like a simple thing to do.

These are things that happen often. Many people undergo things that give them the feeling, "Wow! Someone came into my mind and he called a second later!" Or, "I had a question and suddenly I saw a kind-of answer right in front of my eyes on a billboard! Wow!"

It happens to everyone, but people think what a coincidence! If you change "coincidence" to "a sign received from the universe, from God, from creation"—and you listen—you could go far.

It is also possible not to understand. That is something that I have recently learned.

I once felt that I had to understand everything, so I studied and immersed myself deeply in knowledge. Lately, I've realized that I will not always be able to understand. This is fine. I just need to trust—trust God, trust my inner self, trust my intuition—even when I do not understand. I need to release control, because needing to understand is actually the expression of a desire to be in control.

That is amazing, because you are actually in control of so many things, yet still, you succeed in releasing the need for control.

Because I have realized I can't always understand the whole picture. It is so vast, so wide in scope, that we stand as nothing compared to it. There is a divine order.

What Is Your Unique Frequency?

In the days between our meetings, I would go back in my mind and process what Shari had said. I found that her beliefs and concepts became more and more understandable to me as I rolled them over in my mind. Not just on a cognitive level, but on emotional, mental, and bodily levels as well.

While Shari and I share many similarities, there are also many differences between us—and that is why I have been able to learn so much from her. Not just me, of course, many others can do so as well.

We should not seek out dissimilarity, but, rather, seek out all that we have in common, and everything that can advance us.

Have you always sought the commonalities? Have you always known we are all one? I asked Shari.

Yes. I was never able to understand why a separation exists among people. Growing up as a girl in Israel, it was mainly the nerds versus the cool kids. For example, I had a friend who was a ballet dancer who dedicated all her after-school time to ballet. So as far as the other girls were concerned, she was different. With me, it wasn't like that. I was everybody's friend.

In America, separation was much more evident. There you often had completely separate social groups. When I was twelve, I was at a public school where there was a group of Latinos who would come to school with heavy chains, "ready for war." There was a group of African-Americans, with Afro hairdos, which were then in style. They would put razor blades in their hair.

I was amazed. And they were allowed to come to school like that?

No one knew. They would hide the razors in case they had a fight with someone who tried to pull their hair; the hair-puller would get cut.

There was the "hippy group," which I was one of, the "shanti." We wore jeans, with embroidered "Peace" and "Love" T-shirts. There were the nerds, their noses always buried in books. And then, outside of school, around the neighborhood, there were groups of bikers who rode Harley-Davidsons.

Of course, I was everybody's friend. As a young girl, I could never understand why this group argued with that group, and why they couldn't stand to be with each other. I hung around with everyone.

I tried to imagine Shari among these different groups. To me, it seemed like something from a movie. It is very different from the environment in which I had grown up. My imaginings brought a shy, pensive smile to my lips. Shari smiled too.

Yes, I have experienced much in my life. Even today, I still try to live life as fully as I can. I try to look at everything from different angles. So, too, do I keep exploring myself, which is how I explore life. I do it out of a sense of mission. This inner-personal exploration is actually a mission, and my mission is to do good. Each insight I receive, every realization, and every change I make, I immediately pass on to private people, or to business, or to social organizations.

And where does this mission come from? Is it something you were born with?

It is the reason I came here—from my first day in this world. It is hardwired into me.

I feel that it isn't merely that you want to do good, but that this need to do good is burning inside you, I said to Shari. And, in this, I identified with her because I feel the same.

Look, just lately I came across a situation that broke my faith and my will to do something for someone, for the nation, for the world. That situation lasted for some time, at least until I felt the sense of mission growing within me once again. I realized that such crises come by on purpose to help me make a renewed choice; to further empower my will to do good and bring good into the world.

Those who have a mission endure many things, many trials and tribulations, with each one further strengthening their mission and their will to bring about a better world. It is a part of who I am. It is inseparable from me."

And how do you pass along this mission? How is it fulfilled?

Through the years, it has manifested itself in my actions and undertakings to bring change into the business world, to philanthropic and spiritual organizations—to bring the world of the spiritual and the conscious into the material world through tangible actions. Today, I understand that what is most important is mainly the energy that we resonate.

I asked Shari to elaborate. I was learning that there are concepts that were utterly clear to her, concepts she was born with, as she said, but I wanted to be sure I completely understood what she meant.

We all have energy. Even without getting into the subject of quantum physics, you can understand that we are all energy. We project energy. We each have our own individual frequency, our own sound. It isn't conscious, but we pass these frequencies to one another. The more I purify my frequency; the more spiritual work I do by removing shells, quieting the concerns, the fears, anger, judgment, and blame while building purity and light inside myself, the more I resonate this outside of myself. If I resonate fear, that fear passes on to the people around me and resonates even farther.

That is also what the Council of Six has been telling me, I thought. The guides say that magnetism always works, but what magnetizes with the greatest intensity is our inner frequency.

When I am connected to fear, fear is what I will echo. When I am connected with the belief that I will be successful, success is what I will echo. It isn't only the universe that reacts to our echoing. We, too, sense these frequencies. Think

about how you feel while talking to someone. You can sense the frequency they are on. Sometimes you don't even need to be talking to that person. It can be enough for one to stand beside them to feel their energy; their inner echoing. I wanted confirmation of my thoughts from Shari.
So, we can actually feel the energy around us?

Exactly. We feel each other's energy and project it to each other. When you change your energy—not just your thoughts, your feelings, or your actions—people sense that. Energy that is more purified, that is cleaner and gentler, will pass to others and open their hearts.

There is an energy that will shrivel and limit, and a different energy that opens and widens. There is an energy that belittles, and an energy that empowers. These energies are things we sense in each other, but we do not talk about them, or understand them.

So, when you understand something inside yourself, and create peace or serenity, or have a realization, your frequency changes and transmits a different influence?

Yes. For example, if someone comes to a meeting in an agitated state, angry, and begins yelling at everyone, a defensive atmosphere is immediately set up.

Everyone becomes stressed.

There is tension and the meeting will be chaotic. However, should I come into that room and ask everyone to take a moment to sit quietly and meditate together, to relax and remove all their pressures from themselves, then the atmosphere in the room will soon become peaceful.

The process can be verbal or non-verbal, but it is something that we sense in each other.

I thought about this concept being significant for parents, too. If I change my frequency, I influence my children differently.

As if she were reading my thoughts, Shari continued.

I say to people, "If you do not believe in your child, they can sense it."

Energy, even if it isn't verbal, changes in all circles of life. I think that an important thing we, as humans, must learn, is the influence that our individual energy has on others.

I talk a lot in terms of "think good, speak good, do good" because it is simple to understand; but even that is complicated for some people. Actually, it is about the energy we project.

I recalled how I once gave a workshop for mothers and their young daughters, who were about twelve. The subject of the workshop was body image. Amazingly enough, the girls knew precisely, not only what their mothers thought about their daughters' bodies, but also what the mothers thought about their own bodies.

They knew this, even without the mothers ever talking about it directly. This was especially surprising in homes where there was not open communication about such subjects between mother and daughter. Even so, the frequency had been projected from mother to daughter.

I am aware that my own children have always known what I think and feel about essential matters, even when I try to act differently if I am afraid they might do something that will not work for them.

That syndrome mainly appears when fear or concern is involved. A lot of feeling is wrapped up in fear and concern, making the frequency of feeling much more powerful than during ordinary thoughts. When I am afraid something bad might happen, that is what I project for others to sense.

If I think good, I will project good energy. If I think bad, I am unable to project good energy, and this affects others.

Right. One of the best proofs of this was discovered by a Japanese researcher. He found that if you bless (or curse) water—if you express love or hate toward it—the molecules of the water change. About seventy percent of the human body is water, so it, too, is similarly influenced on the molecular level. That is the energy that passes. That is what echoes in our bodies. That energy literally changes our particles, our structure.

That makes it even more significant, because I have no control over that influence. If you are near to me with good energy, it will change the structure of my energy, or at least have an influence on me. Similarly, if you are in a state of bad energy, no matter how hard I try, I will be negatively influenced by it.

Yes, unless you learn to strengthen your energy. To do this, think of a sun, for example; a sun that is bright and glowing. This will strengthen your energy, and it will be more difficult for the bad energy to penetrate (but most of us don't go around all day long acting as if we are the sun).

Right.

We are a little cloudy sometimes, or rainy, or just a little bit sunny. Any of these makes it easier for unwanted energies to get in. If we understand that our changes influence the whole world, if we truly understand that, then we become more responsible for what we think, what we say, what we do, and how that resonates.

Because we are always resonating.

Exactly.

I admired Shari's words.
This is actually a part of your mission, I said. To bring that understanding forward; to adapt it and present it to everyone at eye-level.
Shari nodded in agreement.
And this book is a part of that resonating? I asked.

Yes. When I read your book, I knew that I had to get to know you. What I liked about the book was that you were able to take things that were known to me and put them into writing in a simple and readable way that will appeal to anyone, to everyone. I immediately knew we had a shared mission.

I smiled and I felt a little bit of joy leap into my heart, because I felt the same.
Shari, what would you wish for the person who reads this book?

In everything I have done, including this book, I wish for people to begin on or to continue their journey along the path. I do not say how, or which path, but they should go down that path that leads them to themselves; to connect better to their souls, to their divine spark—that they begin to know themselves, grow, and become better people, better citizens of this planet. It will follow then that they, themselves, and their environment, will become better; everyone will be better—more good.

I want this to be a book that comes from the soul in a simple, clear way. I want a bridge to form between the mind and the heart from both of our souls to all other souls. That is what this book is about.

I looked at her and felt the connection between us—soul to soul—with no gaps—without differences, and with lots of love.

How Do You Differentiate Between Identity and Essence?

As had become usual, Shari and I were sitting in her office, side by side, on the couch that had become familiar and comfortable to me. Our conversations always began with our sharing of the significant experiences we had gone through since we last met. We talked about our children and families, and then got back to us; the personal growth of each of us, and the insights we had during our time of absence.

I shared with Shari the confusion I had felt during the past week. In one moment I felt significant. I was able to touch people, generate change, and was surrounded by love. In the next moment I felt all that I am yet to be. I experienced the gap in me; the gap between who I want to be and who I am.

I am much more than who I am.

As Shari said this, she had an understanding smile on her lips.

I looked at her, surprised. I opened my mouth to speak, but she continued on before I could ask her what she meant.

"I" is energy, "I" is mind, brain, feeling, body, DNA. The "I" is not Shari Arison, sixty, mother of, grandmother of, daughter of, businesswoman, philanthropist. That is very narrow. People nowadays have a sort of "business card" of who their "I" is. But this is so too narrow a definition, because "I", is as wide as the world.

I once heard a rabbi say that when a person presents himself as a doctor, professor, lawyer, or businessman, it sounds as if that title has some great significance. But, he said, it is a very narrow definition because the person presenting himself as a doctor is also a father, a husband, a son. Is he also a brother? Is he an artist in his soul? He is a million more things.

Even our gender is too narrow a category. I am a woman. I am a man. Right. In this life I am a woman, but my soul, the divine spark, resides inside me. And there, there is no gender; no male or female—no motherhood, even.

I am a mother in this life. Thank God. It is a blessing, and I love the role, but it is only a role; it does not define me. There are so many other things inside me that make up my essence that no title can represent the complete picture of who I am.

Right, I thought. What had pained me during the past week was the fact that I had been trying to define who I am through my actions. I realized that my definition of myself included only a narrow observation of a particular aspect, just as Shari had said.

Once again, I asked her to elaborate.

I think it is ridiculous to say that we know someone, especially in today's digital world. You look at someone and judge them through the media, their looks, or their actions; and, by the way, that person isn't even familiar with their own aspects.

You can continue to learn about yourself your whole life. I have been learning about me all my life. I have spent the last forty years studying my internal processes. It is never-ending and will continue even after my death. So how can anyone say they know me? They know only the illusion they see.

Or they know only a part of you, I said, feeling a little ashamed because that was exactly what had happened to me when I first met Shari. But you are not your image, I said.

Correct, I am not my image. And it is even more extreme in my case, because I am a public figure. People feel they know me, but they don't.

I could hear pain in Shari's voice, and I, again, found myself swaying from side to side in my thoughts. I felt sadness, because she was the icon, Shari Arison, who people were quick to judge by looking for selfish motivations in her actions.

I thought about the suspiciousness that existed in me, and, possibly in us all. Once more, I felt that the differences between us worked to my advantage. When I share something—an experience, a dream I wish to fulfill, or simply something personal—I feel that people not only listen to me, but encourage and embrace me with warmth and support. What happens when Shari shares things with others in this way? Do they respond in the same manner?

I felt that a significant question had surfaced there. I realized that it was not Shari who was the issue. How I relate to her reflects how I relate to myself, and to the world. Just how open am I about getting to know my real self and my own skills? How open am I about getting to know the Shari who is beyond the stigma? Was I not my own harshest judge and critic? I was the one who paid attention to every mistake, to every single thing that failed to work for me. Aren't most of us like that? First and foremost, our judgment is turned inward, and only then is it turned externally, toward others.

Shari continued.

There are very few people who know me well. I can count them on the fingers of one hand. And even among those who do know me, they do not always truly know me. I have beloved friends who have accompanied me throughout my life, and I am aware that even they do not know me thoroughly.

What does it mean to truly know someone? That's a big question. But a more important question is, do I know myself? Do I see myself even before others can see me?

That was it! Shari made a significant point. How willing am I to see my own self in all my different shades and colors? I felt a tightness in my stomach. What was this realization that scared me so? Was it the possibility that I might see things I did not like? Or could it be that it was actually the fear of seeing an inherent strength in myself? A greatness unique only to me? I felt fear rising again.

I'm not sure that I know myself fully. I keep finding out new things, I said.

Self-learning is a process that takes a very long time, and, even then, we do not really know ourselves, because always throughout our lives, we continue to find out more and more about ourselves. Even when someone close tells me, "I know you," I always think to myself, how can you know me, when I have just discovered something new about myself?

Sometimes people think they know me because they had been a part of my life ten or more years ago. They don't. Today I am someone completely different. I have changed. There are those who would say it is impossible to change, but even when a person does not want to, and doesn't even work at it, they still change.

You keep changing all the time?

Yes, all the time, even if you are not aware of it. But a person who wants to change, and works on it, and undergoes processes, they can change in wonderful and miraculous ways.

People are convinced they know someone. They stamp them with a particular stigma and cement it. They do this to themselves as well, staying stuck in themselves. And even if that thing were true for a single moment, that moment is fleeting and has already passed. A person is always changing. Constantly.

This is even more true for a public figure. Of them, we only know what we see on television, on Facebook, in pictures, or elsewhere. Still we take a stand, passing judgment, and we build a story around that person, especially if there is gossip involved. The story gradually expands to include more and more circles, and people think that the story is the truth. They do not know the facts, the person, their actions, or who they really are, but there is judgment. There is an image. And that is what people see and think."

I wholeheartedly agreed with Shari. Before I met her, the little that I knew about her had come from the media. It had all seemed true to me then. I know today that such reports are not always accurate, and that most people are different from the public, media-created image they are stamped with.

But, what interests me more is our ability to get to know ourselves in all our different facets.

What happens when you fail to recognize who you truly are?

If I do not recognize who I am, how can I expect others to recognize me? How can I expect others to see me if I do not truly see myself? Do I see my true self, or do I see only my image? Do I see what I was taught—my habits, my patterns, my feelings, my thoughts?

I have done a lot of self-observation. But still, is this who I really am? My thoughts and my feelings? No. Most people do not know themselves. They also do not know themselves beyond their shells; it is their shell that they think portrays them. They think that their thoughts, feelings, patterns, beliefs, gender is who they are, but that's not who they are. It's not who we are. It is who we were trained to be and who we have become accustomed to being.

So, who am I really?

Whenever I am asked who I am, I invariably say that I am a soul inside a body—and that body, at this moment, is Shari Arison.

But what does that mean?

That, I do not know!

Who Am I in All the Circles of Life?

My conversations with Shari were always fascinating. I relished the opportunity to get to know new facets of her, to see her vulnerable side living in harmony with the powerful side. She was sometimes very sure of herself, while at other times she was not so sure—just like me.

Our conversations helped me to see who I was from different perspectives and to understand things differently. I drew a significant insight that one of the things that had been most stopping me from progressing in life, preventing me from being as much at my best as I would have liked, was because I had always viewed myself from a permanent set of perspectives. I regularly judged myself in the same manner; being angry about the same things, being disappointed again by what disappointed me over and over. I suspect that it is like that with many of us.

I had a thought! Perhaps, instead of fighting it, I could simply change the perspective from which I viewed myself? Maybe then I would be able to view things differently?

Wow! This was exactly what my guides had been telling me again and again—that how I am willing to see myself creates the way in which others see me. That is the ex-

act opposite of what I had once thought. I thought if I became successful, others would see me as successful—and so would I!

The guides explained that, energetically, it works the other way around. Until I saw myself as successful, others would not be able to see me in that way because my frequency is transmitted to the others.

While this is not about the people closest to me (who are able to see the beauty in me even when I am less successful), but about the wider world. I'm talking about the people who do not know me at all, or who know very little about me.

How do you create that state, then? I asked the guides. How do you feel successful, beloved, significant—or any other thing?

You simply stop for a moment and feel that way, the guides replied.

Just like that? I asked, confused.

Yes. Stop for a moment and allow yourself to feel beloved, embraced, wanted, significant. Do not judge it, but simply be there three times a day, just for a moment or two, and things will change.

Despite sensing that this process could work, I felt resistance within me. How could that be it? How could it be something so simple? I was only to imagine it, and it would happen? The rational side of me rebelled. I felt I needed a different course of action; however, despite my doubts, I promised myself I would do as the guides suggested.

I adopted the guidance of the guides, and it worked wonders for me. The change it generated in me has been enormous. In my courses, I now teach their process and I completely understand that the frequency we transmit about us influences the opinion of others . When a person believes in themself, it makes it easier and more convenient for others to believe in them, too. If someone does not believe in themself, why should others?

I had learned that Shari constantly asks herself questions. She observes her life. She repeatedly re-examines everything that happens to her, including her behavior and reactions, and she learns much by this.

I knew that Shari would be able to help me find a practical way of self-observation that would empower me. I asked her to share with me the questions that would help me to better understand who I really am.

You need to ask yourself whether you are the same person, the same essence, in all the circles of life? Am I that when I am alone, when I am with my partner, when I am with my children together, with each child individually, when I am at work, in public, and when I am in the community? These are the questions of essence that anyone can ask.

How is my sleep? Do I wake up in the morning after a quiet, good night's sleep? Do I suffer from insomnia? Do I remember my dreams? Do I see, hear, and travel in them? I think that much can be learned from the world of sleep. I am in the process of exploring this. Myself, I travel in my sleep and I have conversations while I'm asleep—and I get up tired.

What do you mean by travel?

The different dimensions—and all times: past, present, and future—they actually exist simultaneously. If I look at a timeline, and I am situated in the present, it appears to me as if a past and a future exist both behind and in front of me. If I hover above the timeline, I can see all times. I can also rise up through the dimensions in the same way you can take an elevator from the first to the hundredth floor, and the perspective is different from each floor. I find that my development does not stop, not even for a single moment; that, even during my sleep, I travel through various perspectives. Yet, even if it takes me time to understand what I see, I still learn from it."

So, a quiet night is actually not as good?

I would like to say that I have had some peaceful, quiet nights—and especially to be less tired. Still, I believe we undergo what is right for us, both day and night.

You spoke about the dimensions we experience. What kinds of questions can a person ask themselves on that subject?

What is my experience of my own dimensions? Is there only a single, earthly dimension, here and now, or not? Which dimensions do you see and experience? Describe the spiritual experiences. Do you see, hear, believe, know, smell, and feel? Do you have physical sensations in the different dimensions? These are the essential questions you can ask yourself.

My thoughts turned inward, to myself. I do not "travel" when I sleep at night. I do, however, travel during the day-time when I am channeling. Many times, I feel as if I am roaming the world of the beyond. I talk to souls, I sit down to have conversations with the guides. During this activity I always visit the same expanse. However, Shari spoke about dimensions in the plural. I wanted to understand.
You experience several dimensions?

That is something that is hard to explain, because it is something I experience and see. I know that there are others, as I do, who experience and see similarly.

Just as you perceive a dimension of time, everyone senses that there are occasions when time seems to moves very slowly, and other times when you get the feeling that time is running; is moving very quickly. These are the different dimensions of time.

In one country, the sense of time is different from another. I find that in each country I travel to, the sense of time is different for me. Is this because of my business and what I am doing there? Sometimes it is; sometimes it really isn't.

Sleep is when I am able to feel the dimensions the most. I dream a lot and I experience my travels in the dimension of time because I can actually see myself. For example, I can be in a different house, with people, some of whom I know, but, in the dream they might be playing other roles—a friend, a mother, a father—so I must have traveled to a different incarnation, to a different time dimension.

So, the dimensions represent the changes we undergo in various situations?

It is a sensation, like waves, offering us a completely different experience. In our consciousness, we can reach any dimension—our past, our reincarnated past, our future. We can see potential futures and open new horizons.

Think about movie theaters. Entering one theater you might watch a romantic movie and call it dimension one—movie theater one. In movie theater two a comedy is being screened. There is a horror movie in theater number three and a drama in four. I can choose a theater showing a movie in English, Hebrew, Japanese, or French.

When we open and broaden our horizons, we see things in a much wider perspective. We pass through the various dimensions of time and the dimensions of consciousness that are at different levels, different frequencies, and of different densities, because there are dimensions that are extremely dense and other dimensions that are airy.

Ask yourself this questions. Discover where you are. Only when you know where you are and are open to discovering something new—and allow space for this—only then will discovery take place.

So, we all experience different dimensions, but not everyone is aware of this?

Yes, for one person, a dream will be nothing but a dream. It is not real. For another, it will be a trip to a different dimension where they receive insights and messages. It is all a question of how open you are to discover, to hear, to see, and to broaden your horizons.

People are sometimes not open to this because they resist the semantics—the words. I ask myself questions that anyone can ask to themselves. Do I have intuitions? Am I channeling? Do I see? Do I hear? Do I listen? These are questions of internal introspection.

However, for many people a question such as, do you believe immediately arouses resistance instead of a genuine yes or no answer. I believe in the Creator. I believe in God. I believe in the universe. I believe in myself—in my internal aspect. I believe in logic. I believe in keeping my feet firmly on the ground. All of these answers are good and they are genuine. I urge people not to get stuck on the semantics.

Words such as "intuition" or " channeling" generate objections. Some people will immediately say, "No, I don't channel, but my heart tells me that . . . ." or, "An idea popped into my head."

I am aware of people who channel regularly, who possess knowledge beyond the here and now, but they do not allow themselves that moment of introspection to see where it comes from. It frightens them so much that they reject it outright. I urge people to investigate, to be more open, to not get stuck in their exploration because of a particular word or because objections arise from it. We all have our own words.

So, you are saying to remain in your experience, in what is happening to you? Seek to understand what you are going through without rushing to put it into words and definitions?

Yes. Above all, keep your mind open. If this book poses questions that will be suitable for some people and jolt others, instead of resisting and pushing them away, explore them. Ask, Why do these questions jolt me? What is this doing to me? Where does it come from? That is the process of internal introspection. Through internal introspection we are able to discover how we can attain knowledge.

Is everything truly rational? Is there something in me beyond the rational? Is this something I feel in my heart? Is it something I feel in my body? Do I hear voices? Do I see images?

And such knowledge can truly be totally rational?

Yes, definitely. We are each built differently. We constantly compare ourselves with one another. It does not matter that we each possess unique fingerprints. We want to be the same or to be exact opposites; either/or.

In nature, however, there is a vast variety; there are many animals, a huge range of fruits, vegetables, plants, and trees. Each of them is unique and unlike the others. Human beings are the same. We are a part of nature. We have many different varieties.

In order to know ourselves, we have to explore ourselves. Once we understand ourselves it becomes much easier to understand the others around us. It is when we accept ourselves that it is much easier for us to accept those around us. When we love ourselves it is much easier for us to love all others.

So, the questions we have been asking ourselves are intended for introspection and they have no one, single answer. These are questions for inner observation.

Yes. The answers we get may be clear-cut, or they may be true for a particular moment, and then will change over time. The answers might well be precise for the person who has asked them, but not necessarily be true for someone else.

So, there is no single truth?

I think that, eventually, everything does become connected, because there are many shades to the truth; for each their own shade and for each their own color, but, ultimately, we are all connected in some sort of rainbow.

We change our consciousness perspective all the time. We simply do not call it a different dimension. For example, when I am sad, I am in a state of low consciousness. Then, a moment later, something occurs that makes me happy, and I feel my spirit uplifted and expanding. My consciousness changes, and, with it my whole perspective—and my view of the world also changes.

There is no single truth, just different angles of observation. They are all connected to a larger truth that we are normally able to see only small parts of. It is like two people looking at the same person, with one having a front view while the other sees the rear. They provide two completely descriptions of the same person.

Furthermore, even were two people to look at the same person from the same angle, they would still perceive and describe that person in different ways. Which of them is correct? Both, of course! Each will focus on different details that are part of the same person.

This also happens with intuition, channeling, and with connecting to guidance. We may receive different answers from different channelers. Each channeler will provide a different angle to the message received. Of course, that does not mean any of them are wrong. They are all right, and they are all connected to the truth.

You can describe the whole world, the Earth, even the different universes, as pieces in a giant jigsaw puzzle. Only when you put all the pieces together do you see the larger, complete picture. Each part of the puzzle has a unique size, shape, and color. Joined together, they form the complete and larger picture. Most people in the world are unaware that they are a part of such a larger picture.

What do you mean by "larger picture?"

When I talk about the larger picture, I mean that I am, first of all, a human being. Within that picture, that whole entity of human being, there are many different components: the brain, internal organs, circulatory system, tissue, and nervous system. I have arms and legs and a body. Then there are my feelings, emotions and sensations; my thoughts, and my energy. My energy centers are my chakras. I have a halo, and I am a part of an energetic network that connects all humanity.

And that is just a drop in the ocean. Each of those components—and many others—are like pixels that make up an image. They are a part of the larger, complete picture that is myself. But I, too, am only a pixel within the larger picture that is the earth. Every person is a pixel, along with the animals, the plants, and Gaya, an entity unto itself—the energy, the air . . . .

And then there is the moon, the sun, and the stars. These, too, are pixels that make up the solar system, which, in turn, is a part of the larger picture of the galaxy. Even the galaxy is merely a part, a pixel, within the larger universe. All is one pixel in a larger picture composed of all universes—a "multiverse"—a picture that we might choose to call "The Creator."

But most people see only a very narrow picture—me and my partner, the children, work, troubles, feelings, things that make me angry. They see "me" and they see "my survival," but these are just tiny spots. They are only pixels in a larger, complete picture.

It isn't just about space, but also about time—because we are here, in our bodies, only for the mere blink of an eye.

I had never thought about it like that. For some reason, it both amused and comforted me. We truly are specks in the universe; but for me, we are still the most meaningful speck there is—us and all that surrounds us.

Perhaps it is precisely because we are a speck on the one hand, and so significant on the other, that makes it so important for us to live our current lives the most positive we can, so we can feel that we are living in self-realization and fulfillment.

However, for that to be reality, it is important that we thoroughly and deeply, get to know ourselves and what is truly important to us. Observation and asking questions are excellent ways of getting to know who we really are.

That said, it seemed challenging to me to think about these things on my own.

What if I am unable to find the answers? Why can't I simply go to a teacher who can explain all these things to me? What is the advantage of doing this on my own, or of doing it over and over?

You don't have to do it on your own. Every person can do this in their own way. You can go to a teacher or a workshop. You can read a book or look for information on the Internet. You can go to a group meeting or choose to have one-on-one sessions. There are countless methods, all of which are perfectly fine. To each their own way.

Whether you choose to be aided by another, or continue on your own, you must remain connected to yourself. There are many external stimuli and recommendations and methods.

When you are connected to your intuition, it helps you to feel what is suitable for you and what isn't. It can even aid you about which teacher is calling to you. You can feel whether it is right for you to work through the process on your own. The moment you get to know yourself, you will find you have the answers.

You can, of course, ask why you should do all this in the first place. For me, it has always been something larger than myself. I am simply built this way. It is a part of my essence and of who I am. I have always wanted to improve myself and improve the world, and it has always been obvious to me that the two things go together. The more I develop, discover and become more empowered, softer, and more loving, the more I am able to influence the world. You ask if this is tiring? I won't lie to you. The process often tires and drains me. But still, I can't stop; in the same way that I cannot stop being who I am.

Each of us needs to ask ourselves whether we should be more introspective; if this is suitable for us, if we want to improve our quality of life, and whether or not we would like to help to make the world a better place. If one has no desire to improve themselves or the world, then these questions are irrelevant, but I deeply believe that everyone wants that. All of us want something better.

So, asking yourself these questions can get you to a better place? First with yourself, and then with the larger world?

Yes. And you don't need to answer all the questions at once. You can work with just a few of them at a time—each with the number most suitable for them. There are those who will answer the questions and meditate, while others will read them and put them aside. Then, in perhaps ten years' time, the questions will suddenly resurface, and you will want to delve more deeply into them. There are those who will find only some of the questions relevant; others who will find all of them relevant—or, perhaps, just one. All of those responses are fine. Each person and what is suitable for them.

For example, I have had to cope over many years with different aspects of myself that were in conflict—wanting and not wanting. So, what do you do with that? You must simply recognize that there is duality; things that exist simultaneously.

What can I do about these conflicts? I accept the inner struggle. I observe it, and I act only when I reach a state of internal peace. When I know for certain that the decision has come from a complete and peaceful place, then I will know it is right for me.

I have lived with duality for most of my life. I think the whole world is dual by nature. We are, all of us, dual—right and left, beginning and ending, day and night—contrasting opposites exist in everything, but I had to become familiar with my inner duality, familiar enough to see it. For years it was a part of me, yet I had been unable to see it at all. It was only after I became aware that there was a duality in me that I was able to accept it.

In this current era we are passing from the old age to a new one. We are passing from a matrix of duality and struggle to wholeness; to light. We are bringing this wholeness to the here and now. I feel I am already there. I am no longer in duality. I find myself more and more in a state of one.

As Shari spoke, everything seemed clear to me. I, too, feel there is a duality in me. I sometimes experience completely contradictory feelings. On one hand I believe; on the other I am apprehensive. On one hand I feel myself as strong; on the other I feel weak.

A moment later, after reconsidering, I felt unsure that this was what Shari had truly been referring to.

What is it exactly that you call duality?

The contradictions inside us. I love and I do not love. I want and I do not want. Someone can become tired of working at a certain workplace, for example. They want to leave, but at the same time, they don't. Or perhaps there is a married couple who know they want to divorce, but they also don't want to break up. I want to go on a diet, but a minute after making the decision, I eat a whole tub of ice cream. Someone wants to quit smoking, but has a cigarette a second later. There are people who want to have children, but don't. They want to have children but feel that perhaps this isn't the right time. Perhaps not now . . . .

In many situations in life we have an inner struggle between desire X and desire Y. That is the duality that exists in us. We want peace, but, also, all too easily, we become militant. Why? These are situations of inner duality.

But duality is a part of our nature. Think about politics, for example. People talk in terms of right and left. If you look at the human body, we have a right arm and a left. Do we cut off our left arm because only the right arm should be the one we use? Or the reverse? We need to realize that we are a single body—that both right and left are necessary. We must look at things as whole; as one.

Ugh! This all sounded so familiar to me.

How many times have I found myself wanting and not wanting something at the same time? Sometimes I want something, but I am afraid of it—this is also a duality, I thought. And what about doubt?

Since entering the world of channeling, I find myself capable of believing and doubting at the same time. Things I am unable to explain have happened, and the realistic aspect of myself begins to ask questions.

My greatest doubts have involved whether to believe the messages I was receiving receive. I cannot hear the guides, and I sometimes cannot see them either. I just, somehow, know they are present. I feel them. And then the question arises in me: has this all been in my head, or is it real?

In the past I have always been afraid of making a fool of myself, afraid of believing, only to discover, later, that it had all been an invention of my imagination.

Is believing and doubting at the same time also a duality?

Certainly. On one hand you believe, and that belief gets us to a certain level . Faith is a kind of forward motion that leads us to something new, but feeling doubt leaves us behind.

Is there a point at which duality ceases? I was hoping that Shari would say yes, although I also thought she wouldn't. It seemed to me that human beings will always harbor colliding, contradictory aspects of themselves; that, perhaps, it is the natural state of things. Or maybe it isn't?

There is a world, a dimension, that is not dual. When we develop, we can reach a transcendent ascension, a state we call enlightenment. It is a connection to the soul, a connection to the Creator. There, no duality exists. Everything is one. Everything is light. But here, we still live in a dual dimension.

The more we broaden our consciousness, the more we elevate it and the more we can transcend duality to be in a state of wholeness. With the work and self-development that I have been doing, and still do, duality lessens.

When I realized that I had dual states, I decided to empower my will, empower my faith, my optimism, and my hope. I became determined to release everything that does not allow duality, that opposes and contradicts it, that is dual to it. I sought to release the fear, the doubt, the immobility—everything that does not allow me to dwell in a state of wholeness and illumination.

So, you are saying that most people who are still in a state of spiritual development experience duality?

Yes.

Is there a way of reaching a temporary state of inner peace while the process of development is going on? Because, in the day-to-day, I feel I am not there yet. How can I create a state of inner peace today, before I strive to reach a state in which there is no more duality?

It is possible. First, you need to recognize a situation in which you want and do not want something at the same time. Then you must recognize that there are opposing parts of you; one part that wants something, and another that does not. The moment you recognize and accept this, you achieve a state of inner peace.

Acceptance and recognition, I repeated Shari's words in my mind.
Ugh . . . . ! Once again, I felt my own lack of acceptance and the inner struggles I constantly experienced; my wish for a constant state of inner peace and quiet.
Shari says that this kind of peaceful state is created when you realize that there will always be opposing facets and forces in us. I agreed with her, but I had been taught to think this was wrong—that everyone needs to reach a state of

harmony. It is difficult to accept that such harmony can be achieved when you have already accepted the fact that there is no harmony. How does that move us forward?

Once more, I remembered the words of the Council of Six:

"There will always be opposing voices inside you. It is a natural state with humans. The important question is this: which of the voices do you choose to listen to? It is a matter of choice. Here, it is important to use careful consideration and thought. When you choose to listen to a voice that weakens you, ask yourself why you have made that choice. Once you are free of judgment and free of the wish to do what others think is right for you, and listen to what is truly right for you, you will be able to choose more accurately which of the voices inside you should listen and to which, not."

The voices in your head are like a table set with many delicacies. When you take a closer look, you may see there are some dishes that are less to your liking, or some that aren't fresh enough, or even spoiled. The fact is, you can't eat everything. You need to choose what is tastier and better for you.

The same can be said about the thoughts or voices inside. They are there for you to choose from. The more you listen to the ones that are good for you, the stronger you will grow, and the more you will develop. The voices do not necessarily represent truth, but they do represent thought, and the right to choose among them is yours.

Shari must have noticed this inner dilemma reflecting in my expression.

When you have opposing forces fighting each other, this allows only a state of war. If we recognize this and we begin to accept this, to love ourselves and all the opposing aspects within ourselves, something inside us relaxes.

Once that is achieved, we no longer are waging a war. The moment things ease up, you can put more emphasis on your true will and aspirations.

I think that when I begin thinking about character traits, I can say that I'm brave or that I'm afraid, but those emotive terms aren't absolutes. Sometimes I'm brave and sometimes I'm a coward.

We're all brave and we're all fearful. It occurs differently in different aspects and situations.

That I define myself as one thing or another is a mistake That creates the collision, the duality.

That's right, because we all possess everything.

I'm nice, but sometimes I'm not. I'm smart, but sometimes I don't understand things. There might always be a duality there. Both things can occur at once. I can't be permanently happy.

I think we have all qualities and traits, but in different measures. I can be brave more than I can be a coward, as well as the other way around, but I do have both qualities. You need to see this, accept it, make peace with it. Then you can begin to focus on what you really want, and empower it, put more and more light on it, and release those things you want less.

When you spoke just now, I had an image in my mind of two children tugging each other in different directions. They will be unable to get anywhere until they make peace. I will tell them to "just hold hands, and you can go together to wherever you want."

Right again. Take a look at the world we live in. Instead of holding hands and realizing that there is room for all shades and colors; instead of being in a state of unity and harmony with all shades and colors, everyone is tugging in a different direction—their own. That situation does not allow peace; neither internal nor external.

Shari's words offered me strength and an inner sense that everything would be fine. Suddenly, the wish to try and avoid duality seemed amusing to me. It is the most natural thing for a person. Acceptance and understanding, created by personal development, releases duality to create a state of internal peace. That internal peace has a very important role.

That realization is a part of humanity's development. If we work on ourselves we can make our world much better as well.

Certainly. The internal development of each of us is then reflected outwardly in the collective evolution.

So, all the hard work is definitely worth it.

Yes!

We both smiled in agreement.

I sank into thoughts of my own, to order in my head the insights I had gained through her.

Duality exists in every one of us. I understood that, but was I truly willing to accept it? Was I willing to accept the fact that I will be nice sometimes and less than nice at others?

How do you make peace with this duality without feeling you are doing something wrong? I could see Shari nod with empathy.

I think that many people go through an unnecessary process of self-abuse.

For example, if I go on a diet that I am unable to go through with, I'll think, Argh! Why am I like this? Why can't I be more determined? Why can't I control myself? I'm such a nobody.

It is easy for us to criticize ourselves, or to blame ourselves—or someone else. Why does she have to eat a cake right in front of me? It's her fault. We blame ourselves and feel guilty, or we blame someone else instead of seeing that this is simply the way nature works—we have both, a will and a counter-will.

When we can see this without blaming ourselves or someone else, without judging; when we can simply start "seeing" this, to observe instead of blame, and note the places in our lives over which we have a certain will, but a contradictory way of behaving, then we can begin to accept ourselves without unnecessary self-abuse, guilt, and blame.

There are many fewer "collisions" in me today. It is an amazing and wonderful thing. I feel so thankful to myself, to my soul, and to God. However, there have been instances in the past, and even rare moments in the present, during which this duality continues to exist when I am faced with myself or with other people.

There are different aspects of me that collide. I want to express myself, but I know that the person in front of me does not want to listen—is convinced they are right. So, there is a collision in me between the place that wants to express itself and say the whole truth, and the place that knows there is not a sympathetic ear on the other end. Expressing myself would, therefore, be useless. What are you to do then?

There are other times, for example, when I really want to work out, to exercise, but I feel very tired. There is something in me that wants to go for a run, but another side of me knows that I need to rest. What do I do?

These are dualities that are very practical, they are very human. They are things we all cope with, but, most times, we don't observe this inner war. We become angry at someone else, or at one of the voices inside us, until we take a more balanced look and recognize that both voices exist in us. We need to reach a state of inner peace with the opposing voices.

If I go for a run when I'm tired I might sustain an injury. If I don't express myself and keep silent, the anger will accumulate in me and make me sick. The first step in resolving this involves taking a long look at these struggles and asking ourselves what is right for us at this particular moment—and then to stop the struggle between the part that wants something and the part that doesn't. Sometimes the part that wants something will win; other times the part that doesn't will gain the upper hand. Both are fine, so long as we observe both of them and learn to let them go. When we do, suddenly there is no longer an inner strife. You will have accepted the fact that you have both.

I thought about what the Council of Six had told me:
"Will is what motivates human beings. Will always exists. Sometimes it is positive and helps you to advance; sometimes it is negative and will hinder your progress. You often say that you do not want something, but what you truly

want, is not to do, not to accept. You want something to not happen. There is still, however, will involved. Many times, the desire for something to not happen is stronger than the desire for something to happen. The will always triumphs.

"*The will to do something is often in conflict with fear and other inhibiting factors such as beliefs and concerns. These are actually the camouflaged will to be on your guard, to be careful—the will to not get hurt.*

"*When you act the way you want, it is a sign that your will is stronger than your fear.*

"*When you are unable to act, it is a sign that your will and your fear are balanced; or, that your fear is greater than your will.*

"*Often, there is an exposed will and a hidden will. On the surface, you want something, but deep inside you want something else. This is something worth recognizing.*

"*Satisfaction in the current age comes from the feeling that one is moving along the right path. If you feel you have missed an opportunity, there is a will inside you that remains unfulfilled.*

"*It would be worthwhile to create a map of the will's desires. What are the desires acting within you, and how can you focus them? In which places are there opposing desires of the will?*

"*Sometimes, you fail to understand why you are unable to move, and you are frustrated because of this. This is attributable to an internal will.*

"*It is easier to strengthen or to weaken a will than it is to cope with fear.*

"*Once you have strengthened your will, and it can overcome fear, you will be able to begin moving.*

"*There is no such thing as 'I have no will power.' That feeling simply demonstrates that your will lies elsewhere.*

When you say, 'I have no will power,' you are preventing yourself from having the ability to make choices. Just look at the way children who want something will do anything to get it!

"Adults have learned to hold back, to restrain themselves, and to self-regulate. When they wish to move forward and be successful, they have to empower their will.

"Every time you find yourself not moving, remember that not enough will is present to move you forward.

"The absence of will power is a weakening expression that does not help you to advance.

"What takes place in your life is the subtotal of your will's desires, both the conscious and the unconscious, balanced by your fear. That is why it is important that you focus your will."

I related these words spoken by the Council of Six to Shari. She responded:

There is a vast difference between will power and an authentic will. When people speak about will power, they talk about someone who tells everyone that they have stopped smoking; then, five minutes later, they smoke a cigarette. There is also the someone who declares having begun a diet who eats some cake the very same day. Those demonstrate the opposing and conflicting forces within us.

You can overcome them with will power, but unless that will power comes from an internal and authentic place, a peaceful and whole place, then, at a certain point, people break. It doesn't work, it fails.

For many years, I have acted out of my desires to go on a diet, to exercise, or to work hard. That simply brought me to a very exhausted place. At a certain point in my life I chose to let go of all of the things that I supposedly had to do because I possessed will power and I simply stopped going on diets and exercising. I stopped doing things I simply did not want to do.

I made a deal with myself. I would do things that came only out of an inner, genuine, authentic will. True, this took some time, but once I was back to doing things that were correct, that were right for me, I did them with an entirely different level of energy.

For me, this was, once more, an example of Shari working from the premise that she was attentive and listened to her internal will. It is because, when a person listens, things become clear and a state of inner peace is achieved.

I confirmed this with Shari. You act only when you reach a state of inner peace?

Yes, these days I act only when I have reached a state of inner peace. There was a time when urges used to activate me. For example, when I was angry at someone I would quickly rush to tell them what I thought. I did not operate from out of the my quiet place. I am now able to recognize when I am very angry.

Yes, I still have the urge to pour fire and brimstone on the person's head, but I also know that doing so will do no good; it will contribute nothing. So I stop for a moment, I observe, and I refrain from doing anything until I gain the insight I seek.

Sometimes, that insight is simply to wait and to talk only when the other person has become attentive. Sometimes that insight points toward releasing my emotions in the belief that the other person will come to understand on his own.

The insights change from one event to the next, and from situation to situation. It is important to allow a moment for the two conflicting forces to become present inside us in complete opposition—without taking action.

So, we mustn't take an action before some sort of clarity is achieved?

Yes, clarity. The awareness of a certain state of peace, a distinct tipping of the scales to one side or the other.

I sank into deep thought for a moment. I have never been able to force myself to do things. So long as there is an inner resistance I have been unable to progress. I have learned that I need to ease this resistance. It often takes time—and it can be frustrating—but it works.

I had never been able to lose weight when I scolded myself. Only when I learned to accept this as a difficult task, and treated myself lovingly, was the change created.

These ideas brought a smile to my face, and I found myself thinking about Joy, one of the spiritual guides. She is always amused by the illogical senselessness of human behavior.

I heard Joy in my head, saying, "If, when you scold yourself, it doesn't help, and you are thereby unable to get what you truly want, why then, do you keep doing this to yourself—over and over and over again?"

How Do You Distinguish Between Different Energies?

At our next meeting, Shari began the discussion.

Everything I "feel" is mine, but, at the same time, it is not solely my own. It can also belong to the earth, to humanity, to the country, to anything that is currently happening. When we reach a state of high sensitivity, a feeling is both personal and above personal. It is much broader.

We sometimes also experience the feelings of others, do we not?

Yes, but people don't know how to separate their own feelings from the feelings of others. They don't know how to put their finger precisely on the reason. We can feel unwell without knowing why, or be happy without knowing the cause. We can get our feeling states from one another. It's catching. If there is something general or universal that we feel, is it or isn't it ours? Or is it both? We regularly switch energies and energy flows. Sometimes I feel a hard, inclusive, collective, negative energy passing through me.

When I fall into the kind of pit in which I feel a heavy energy, I will first search for a reason for feeling that way. If my health had not been great during that time, then I will assume that is the reason I have been feeling unwell —that feeling unwell is making things hard for me. Feelings of frustration and despair begin to well up until I realize those feelings aren't just mine.

I considered Shari's words. Many times, we feel things that are not our own. We feel someone else's sadness, pain, or distress. Sometimes, when I am in a bad mood, it is because there is someone nearby me who is transmitting some low energies that affect me. I don't always notice this. Sometimes I feel as if such a mood is entirely of my own making. Being aware that this can happen helps. I wondered what Shari does when this happens to her.

How do you realize that some mood, some feeling, isn't your own?

After years of practicing awareness, I have reached the point where I am able to recognize it. I recognize how it connects to something that is low in me, something difficult in me, but that its intensity isn't mine.

When that happens I feel I have a role—to transform those harsh energies into something positive—to transform the darkness into light.

To do that, it is necessary to understand which of our inner narratives the negative feelings are attaching to; which of our inner energies they are connecting with. Then you need to separate each of the elements and determine that this one is mine—this is my story, my narrative, and my energy—and this one is not. Then you need to do some work: to purify, ascend, and cleanse, until you reach a better place.

That is the difference between negative energy and positive energy; the energy of light and the energy of darkness. Negative energy is energy that tries to take over. It fights to take charge. The energy of light, of the positive, is a quiet energy. It is soft and pleasant.

Think about this. Imagine the words "war" and "fight" equate to darkness. When you enter a dark room, all you have to do to make the darkness go away is turn on the light. The energy of the light, of pleasantness, is the energy that transforms.

The energy of struggle and war causes destruction and separation because it is always directed against someone. It is a different kind of energy. The number of times I hear the words "war" or "fight" coming out of people's mouths, about the most trivial things, simply astonishes me.

I "fight" for my son to stay in school. I "fight" to have people talk respectfully to me . . . .

Just think about how tiresome and draining dealing with that energy is.

I think this is also an educational and cultural thing. Here in Israel, you have to fight for everything.

That is understandable. Israel is a country fighting for its survival, but, today, we have reached a point where we can choose differently. We have existed for seventy years now. It is fine to protect yourself, to remain alert and vigilant, but there is no longer a need to do so much fighting. I think that if you fight for your place in the world, that results from not having a place of your own. You can try to attain your place in the world in simpler ways.

We have been educated, to a certain degree, to fight for our right simply to be. Perhaps now, today, it would be better for us to try to do it differently.

In the dual world of right and wrong, left and right, light and darkness, the spiritual process involved is to see the inner war and make peace among all the different parts of ourselves. It is a spiritual work involving exploration, the dismantling of all the ingredients of mind, feelings, soul, and body, and reconnecting them in a comingling of understanding and acceptance.

In the new world being built now, a world called by some, "the second coming," and by others, "the consciousness of the One," we need to release the consciousness's vibration of duality, both war and peace together, so we can reach a state of peace—a peace within the whole, a place where there is no male and female, no parts—where there is merely an energy of wholeness. It is like when a child is embraced by his parents—a place where we are all being embraced by God; a place of safety, of protection and love, and a place where we feel held; a place that allows us to trust and believe . . . . a place in which we can rest.

Are My Interior and Exterior One and the Same?

We were sitting, as usual, in Shari's office, talking about the events of the past week.

I loved and cherished those moments. They offered me a feeling of bonding and intimacy free of judgment. I sensed that Shari was sincere with me, and I was with her. I felt how Shari's public image slowly melted into the background in my mind, and I was able to connect more and more to the person she truly was. The more I got to know Shari, the more I loved and appreciated her. We could talk about anything and everything.

When I shared my feelings with Shari, she smiled.

Because the interior and the exterior are one and the same.

What do you mean by the interior and the exterior are one and the same?

Finding the way to be true with myself and genuine with others, so that the exterior and interior are one. Am I truly able to say to those around me the same things I am saying to myself?

Most people go around wearing masks. Ask a person how they are doing, and they will always say fine, or everything will be all right. No one stops to really tell you what sort of day they've had, or that they have just had a fight with their spouse, or that they are worried about their son.

Maybe in day-to-day chitchat, wearing a mask is the right thing to do?

I'm not claiming that one should say everything they are thinking, but I do think that, as you learn to be truthful with yourself, you will become truthful with the world.

People have always thought that because I am a businesswoman I should behave in a certain way, and behave differently as a spiritual person, and differently again as a family person. To this I have always responded, no, I am who I am. I am myself in every place and in every circle of life.

That said, many people are expected to be different selves in different places. This is expected of them both by themselves, and by others. But, when we connect with ourselves, with who we truly are, our internal aspect is reflected externally everywhere we go, and in whatever we do.

So, again, you are suggesting self-observation. Recognize where you are genuine and truthful, and where you are not. What you dare, and do not dare, to say, without being judgmental about it.

It is perfectly fine not to say anything. Indeed, sometimes it just isn't appropriate. Sometimes I may choose not to share my thoughts with someone because they are not in a place that allows them to truly listen, or to understand, and it simply isn't the right time. The fact that I think something does not mean I have to immediately let it out. Absolutely not. I am simply saying that when you are very precise with yourself, truthful with yourself, then you will generally be precise and truthful with the world. It is then that your interior and exterior are one and the same.

I shared a memory with Shari that I had of my mother, who had been a wonderful, but also quite challenging woman. She could be very blunt sometimes and had screamed at me more than once.

When I became a mother, I promised myself that I would try never to shout at my children, and try not to speak too bluntly to them, or humiliate them.

Over the years, every time I had a confrontation with my children, I found I would freeze and come to a dead-end, unable to say anything more. I now realize that it was fear that had caused me to freeze. I realize that I had not known what to do and I had been afraid that I might become my mother. So I simply stopped.

Now I see that I still stop whenever I don't know how I should act. I prefer to stop because I don't know what is right for me, because sometimes it seems to me that both options are wrong—that it is wrong to keep silent and also wrong to speak out and scold. So I simply postpone the "coping" for a later time, after I come to truly understand what I want to do.

And that was a very good decision. I think we are in a very different age now. Throughout history, human conduct has been based on the fight-or-flight principle. We either avoid doing so, or we fight. As human beings, we know how to do nothing else.

I have found that whenever I reach such a dead-end, whenever I do not know what to do, I simply stop and turn to a power that is beyond myself—God, the Creator, my inner-self, the universe, the energy—whatever name you have for it—and I seek help and guidance. I ask to be shown the way. And I let go. For example, I do this if I want to have a good relationship with someone, and that person keeps on fighting.

And, still, with all the good will in the world, I can't reach the state of love, compassion, and mutual communication I would like to have. I just keep my heart open. I do not shut down. I do not fight. I simply let go and allow the universe to work. I seek help. I seek guidance. I ask for the solution to come to me.

Amazing! The truth is that, on the sorts of occasions Shari was describing, I did not always remember to turn to the guides for help. At that moment I made a promise to myself to remember to do so in the future.

What had earlier typified the previous generation, the previous age, was that not knowing something was forbidden, I summed up. There was no situation in which, if I had not known something, I would have decided to wait for the solution to come. I would not have asked for help nor waited for things to clear up. I had to have the solution in that instant.

For me, I think it is important not to know—to accept that I do not know. Many times, our attempt to know "how" will disrupt our understanding of the "why." These days, I focus on my intent and my will. If I wish to achieve harmony, or anything else in life, the most important thing is to sharpen my will; be in a state of pure intent to focus on what I want, to believe it is possible, to allow it to come, and then to let go.

As Shari spoke, a sense of wonder welled up in me. Our meeting was taking place exactly two days after this same subject had come up during my weekly channeling session. Today, I no longer view such things as coincidences, but as an assurance from the Council of Six of the importance of these things—and as a reinforcement of the connection between Shari and myself.

I am shocked, I told Shari. That was exactly what we talked about in my channeling session!

Shari smiled.

The same thing happened at our previous meeting.

That's right! And it was also what the guides had distinctly said: That change in the world would happen once a change in the consciousness had taken place. That our efforts should focus on changing our consciousness and perspective, and external reality would follow.

Actually, when I change my consciousness, I am creating a space, as if I have moved. And, into that space, a new reality is able to enter.

True.

So, that is precisely what you are saying—that the work is mental. It is a smaller effort than trying to create a physical transformation in reality because you do not know something—then you feel as if you are drowning.

I feel that *doing* is much easier than simply *being*. To stop and do nothing is not a simple thing. You need to be in a powerful state of inner balance, connected to a very powerful faith.

I hesitated before I spoke next.
I feel that there is a gap between us. You are much more of a believer than I am. Perhaps because you believe in yourself much more than I believe in myself. Or you believe more firmly in the power connected to you.

I am less of a believer, yet I know how to feel and sense what isn't working for me. I have tried more than enough times to change reality, only for nothing to happen.

Many people come to me and tell me that they have tried to imagine a change, but that it simply had not worked for them. I tell them, look at your lives, you are who gets to decide. If doing in reality works for you, continue, but, if it doesn't, then there must be something internal that is stopping you. It is a sign that something inside you needs to change—something in your faith, your internal frequency or your essence. Sometimes we try to do things in different ways and simply cannot. That is because the problem lies in our perception, our inner frequency, which does not allow reality to change.

I just want to clarify to say that it isn't that doing is not enough. It would be more precise to say that doing is not always enough. Not in every situation.

That doesn't mean stop acting. We all need to act, do, invest, but it is also about believing, about strengthening your will, and, thus, allowing things to come, but if there are moments when you try as hard as you can, and no matter what you do it doesn't work, that probably means you've reached a point where you need to let go.

I nodded and thought to myself—exactly!

What Is Your "Business Card?"

Shari and I were sitting in her office as usual when I noticed a difference in the way I was feeling. Something in me had changed in relation to Shari. When we had just started our journey together, I regularly felt the gap between us. Not because Shari made me feel it, definitely not, but because I had held on to the self-perception of myself, and the perception of Shari that I had had in my mind.

It had taken me a lot of time to trust that what was taking place between us was genuine, authentic, and that Shari enjoyed my company as much as I enjoyed hers. I needed to be sure that I was enriching her in the same way she was enriching me. I have known that from the very start, but I was unable to feel it, because I had been unable to free myself of judgment.

I thought about how used I was to viewing myself in a particular way. So much so that, even when reality had shown me differently, it still took me some time to process and internalize it. I felt happy over the change I had gone through, and I enjoyed now that I felt a reciprocity between us.

And then, once again, I felt my heart squeeze.

How easily I allowed myself to let go when faced with someone who I felt was similar in position to my own. How quickly did I feel equal to them—and comfortable. On the other hand, how long had it taken me to reach that same comfortable place with Shari? Hand on heart, she had been open and loving with me from the very start. It was I who had difficulty in accepting that openness. Is it possible that many others felt exactly like I did? That we hold a certain image in our minds, both of ourselves and of others—that this image prevents us from being free?

People who ask me who are you expect me to say that I am Shari Arison, a businesswoman, a philanthropist, a mother of four, and a grandmother of six grandchildren. That is my "business card."

But my true business card is that I am a soul. I am an essence undergoing a temporary experience in a human body. That is my real business card.

For most people, their business card will contain lots of external things that have no relation to their true inner selves. Once they realize that, they will be able to start changing it.

Most people view themselves first as a body. Only then do they believe or disbelieve in the soul. This immediately limits them, because they see themselves as a body, as a human being. If you ask me what my business card is, I will tell you that I have always perceived myself as a soul having an experience in a body. These days I know I am a soul who volunteered to enter that body called Shari Arison—who volunteered to enter into this life to bring change into the world, in order to develop, and in order to raise the collective awareness. That is what I was born for. That is my essence. That is my business card.

This is the same way as an actor who goes on stage can portray any character, but when he goes home, he has his own essence—the "him" who he truly is.

For example, if that actor plays a Shakespearian character on stage, when the play has ended, he does not forget to take off his costume and go back to being who he truly is. But some of us, on the other hand, believe ourselves to be the character, and forget our essence.

I have an essence that is mine. I am a messenger, an energy, a soul, a part of God, or Creation. I have come here to this Earth to play a role using this body, with a set of props I was given so I could better play my part. For example, my name, my status, my family, the parents I chose to be born to, the children I chose to have, the difficulties I chose to undergo on my way so I could discover things and develop, become stronger, and grow.

That is my business card. What I suggest that everyone should do is explore and investigate beyond the props they have been given and look beyond the body, beyond the titles, the roles, the gender; beyond I'm a woman/I'm a man/I'm a mother/I'm a father/I'm a lawyer/doctor/author/philosopher/yoga teacher.

Look beyond all these things. It is there that you will find the spark; the innermost essence. What is it? Who is it? Who are you? You will understand that there is something much purer, much deeper, behind the props and the scenery.

I thought that this would be a wonderful exercise—to sort the things I think about myself into props or external things, and then into another group of the things that are genuinely "me." But how is it possible tell the difference?

When you say you are a philanthropist, I see that as something that has an essence in it.

"No. Philanthropist is also a title. The true giving of the essence is like the light of the sun. I am a sun. I give light. Philanthropist is a title, a definition, a person who contributes, builds, supports.

It has the spark Everything I do has the spark from my essence, because my essence is creative. That creativity can manifest itself in art, in writing, in business, or as entrepreneurship, but the essence is the true creation. The others are just definitions.

I think that when you separate these, you can find out who you really are, and that this book is who I truly am. That is the exploration I suggest people do.

I'm going to do it today, I said enthusiastically, as Shari smiled approvingly when she recognized my determination.

Excellent!

However, soon enough, that determination was undermined and replaced by the doubts so familiar to me. I want to do it but, really, what will I gain by it?

I really couldn't tell you.

I wanted so much for Shari to have an answer for me. For her to promise me a "reward" at the end of the process.
What did it give you?

It gave me a lot. When you examine yourself on the basis of a title or a job, there will always be something wrong, something not quite right; that I was or was not successful, or did or did not get something, or was not seen in this or that light. When you are constantly dealing with the external you, it can never compare to who you really are internally. Internally, you are perfect.

Does that mean that this "business card" can help us reach a state of inner peace?

That too. It brings with it a sense of wholeness. It brings inner peace. It brings a recognition of who you really are. It brings, in fact, a lot of things. That is what it brought me personally. Every person who takes the time to search this out for themselves, will discover what it brings them.

I think something good would happen to everyone—to each in his or her own way—they were my thoughts that I spoke aloud.

I'm sure it would. But you need to understand that, often, before you get to all those good things, you need also to experience a lot of things that aren't simple. To see the essence, it is necessary to dispel the things that obscure our sight. In order to do that, you need to be honest with yourself. And, in order to be truly honest with yourself, you need to remove many, many layers; remove them from both your own definitions and your own judgment. You must see not only the things you like about yourself, but also the things you do not like. Then the good will come, but it will be coming from a long way off. It's not simple, but it is possible.

Shari's words persuaded me to pay closer attention to my personal set of definitions over the following days. I had to recognize the times when I was holding on to an external description to cover an inner discomfort. I had to understand when I needed to dispel a layer to reach an inner truth.

I had a feeling that it would be easier for me to see my own weaknesses now. Over the years, I have gradually become more forgiving and accepting of those places in me. The work I do on myself, and I believe, that many of us do, mainly involves observing—noticing when we do not dare to see ourselves in our own greatness.

Admitting and recognizing our strengths is even more frightening than admitting our weaknesses.

How Can You
Clear the Noises?

During one of our sessions, while we were discussing the inner truth that is supposed to guide our way in the world, we agreed that, in order that I act according to my own inner truth, I first had to recognize it. When I asked Shari how this could be done, she responded, through listening.

What do you mean when you say listening? Listening to my inner self? Listening to what is right for me?

It goes far beyond that. It is an observation—a connection with the purest self; clean, authentic, divine, the cosmic. We each have our own name for it, and that is fine. It doesn't matter what you want to call it, but it is an inner connection.

There are stages you must go through, but it starts with listening. To get to the core of the self, most people will have to undergo a journey. We agree that most people in their day-to-day lives are not connected.

Okay, so what does being connected and being attentive to yourself mean?

Look, the brain works like a radio station. It keeps talking—all the time; yattering, yattering, yattering. Ceaselessly. The yattering is our thoughts.

When I truly listen, I begin to discern patterns within that constant noise. I am able to observe the things that are repetitive, and, from this, I am able to understand whether I have an obsession for something. I can establish whether these thoughts are negative or positive; whether they are constructive and empowering, or if they will bring me, or someone else, down. And, I can understand whether they are accepting or judgmental thoughts. Then I can start listening, observing, and discerning what those thoughts are.

The same is true for sensations.

This is done by listening to the body. Is the body comfortable? Is it suffering any pain? Is it stressed or relaxed? Where am I feeling pain? What type of pain is it? Is it physical or emotional?

I might have pain in my legs because I went for a long run and my muscles are sore, or, I could have pain in my legs for no physical, bodily, reason—only because my legs are trying to tell me something. Perhaps they are indicating to me that I should rest because I'm not being sufficiently sensitive to the needs of my body and it needs to rest?

If the pain is a stomachache, was it caused by eating something bad, or is it there because I'm receiving some external energy—that someone said something that hurt me and is causing me to experience some inner tightening?

I have to observe all the parameters of the self; my thoughts, my emotions, my sensations, my body, and my energy—and, through listening, achieve a deeper observance awareness—and through that observance awareness clear away the unwanted noise, whether it be mental, physiological, or emotional. It is then that I will be able to reach a connection with something purer.

These stages, then—observation and attentiveness, realization and connection—they allow us to connect with who we truly are?

Yes. Today, the noises no longer drive me, but in the past, I wasn't always able to reach a state of perpetual connection. That had been my goal, to be connected to my own soul at every moment, to listen to the voice of the soul rather than the background noise—regardless of whether the background noise was internal or external.

Picture a thread, a thin cable, like an electric wire. To connect with your soul, it is necessary to plug this into an appropriate socket. The cable comes from the infinite of the great light above. It passes through the crown of the head, and like a fine, thin tube, the cable continues on through the center line of the body. Thus, there is a connection from the highest-most place all the way from the soul to the physical body. If there is any bad reception that is generated by negative thoughts, beliefs, sensations, or emotions, this pure connection will be disrupted.

If there is a wall, or some kind of armor that I have surrounded myself with as a kind of defense, then there will inevitably be a disconnection that will sever the physical aspect (which is me, the human being) from the divine (which is my soul).

Even when you have attained such a connection, it needs to be constantly preserved, bolstered, and thickened. That is because it is a fragile thread, just at the scale of a single hair, that is capable of carrying the light that passes from the higher regions to the lower ones, but we need to thicken and broaden it until it becomes a tube.

We need to do this increasingly, until there is a genuine flow of light of acceptance and giving; a stream of light emanating from the soul and the Creator that flows outward to affect the world.

I loved the allusion of a cable thickening to become a pipe. Again, this is a concept that fits with the messages I've received.

It seems that the connection to the world beyond, the connection to the inner truth, the voice of the soul, or the guidance from above, is an isolated, one-time experience.

People want me to "open" their channel for them, but it doesn't work like that. The inner voices, external criticism, and even random thoughts about our daily tasks, combine to create a noise that truly disrupts the connection. Even "connected" people have disconnections. The difference is that they know how to reconnect when they want to.

So, when we experience "noises" in our heads, they cause a disconnection? I asked as I shared my conclusion.

Of course. For me it's as if I am trying to tune in a certain radio station and there is background noise causing poor reception. I can't get clear sound or the correct frequency and I continue trying to tune the radio until I find the station. However, I do have to make sure it's the right station, because you can also tune into undesirable stations.

Just as there are people we can connect to and feel comfortable with, there are others we meet and feel uncomfortable with. We need to accept and respect every person, but that doesn't mean that every person is right for us, or is pleasant for us to be with.

The same is true for external frequencies. I can connect, and even receive messages and channelings, but the frequency will not be pure, or one that is directed straight into my soul. To be both connected within oneself, and, at the same time, connected to the purest, most precise place is a skill. Acquiring this skill is a part of the larger process.

What if we are connected only some of the time? Isn't a partial connection still valuable, I asked defiantly, even though, inside, I already knew the answer. Shari replied just as I had expected her to.

Of course it is valuable. Most of us live like this. And, with time, our introspection, self-awareness, and connection to ourselves grows stronger. A person connected to themselves knows what is right for them—that is why this is so important.

What is My Rhythm?

Everyone has their own rhythm, It connects them to who they truly are. Am I fast or slow? When am I fast? When am I slow? My rhythm changes in different areas and in different aspects of life. For example, I understand and utilize new technologies at a very slow pace, but I am very quick to perceive universal, mental, or business-related things—and I am even quicker to act upon them.

Isn't that being judgmental?

It isn't being judgmental. It is a realization. Who am I really? How do I perceive my own rhythm and myself?

How were you able to familiarize yourself with your rhythm?

I actually learned it through others. From a very early age, I have always expected a high level of efficiency from myself and from others; a quickness in performing tasks and getting results.

I am from a family of business-people who have been taught that there must always be an objective, a goal. You assimilate that goal, realize it, and you get results. All in a very quick way.

From the idea, through the vision, to the realization, I have always done everything needing to be done very quickly without realizing just how quick I was, because for me, this has always been natural. People laughingly said that I could easily manage half the world from my kitchen.

I gradually realized that other people were, and are, different from me in that regard. I would ask people for only one thing at a time, not the twenty or fifty simultaneous things I was used to doing myself.

I found that not only were the people I asked to do their one thing occasionally unable to do it, but they also failed to understand the request to assimilate—and, they complained. I was angry about this. I could not understand what the problem was. Why couldn't they do this one thing I asked them to do?

And then, one day, someone asked me to help them with a project. I agreed, and began by running all of the parameters of what would be required for a successful outcome. The woman I was working with said, "My brain doesn't work like that. I don't think the same way you do. I think in a slower fashion. I can do one thing, complete it, and only then can I move on to the next thing."

This was a shock for me. I suddenly realized that what I expected from my environment wasn't realistic. Because I'm fast does not necessarily mean that the person working with me is also fast—that they have the same rhythm as I.

I knew that in nature there are rabbits and turtles, the fast and the slow, but I had failed to truly understand and internalize this. Since then, I have learned to look at people in a different way. I look at myself in a different way too. I understand that I have been blessed with this ability.

I am now able to observe and accept that other people have a different rhythm. We each have our own rhythm of perceptions, of transformation, of awareness, of growth, of realization, and of ideas. I should not try to rush someone, be angry at them, or change them. It is impossible. They simply have a different structure, a different rhythm.

That was a huge lesson for me. It helped me to understand and accept the expectations I have for myself and for others because I have developed this ability. It generated a significant change.

I understand what you are saying, but when I look at myself I have to wonder. Sometimes I have my own rhythm, and other times there are things that obstruct it. How do I know if this is truly my rhythm, or if I'm simply afraid of doing something? If I am afraid, or there is something obstructing me, then, surely, that isn't my natural rhythm.

That is exactly why it is important to make the distinction; to look inwardly to seek to understand the noises that are disrupting the authentic connection. Fear is a type of noise. It is a disturbance. It exists to protect us. The moment we are ready, we can both embrace and release it.

But another significant question is, does an ability exist or not? This isn't about good or bad. It is just like being tall or short. It is simply a neutral, natural given; a part of who we truly are. You, like everyone else, have your rhythm, the rhythm of who you truly are. There can be many things, not just fear, that might cause that rhythm to change sometimes.

For example, perhaps I have a quick rhythm, but I now simply want to rest for a while? So long as I know that I have such an ability, I know not to judge anyone else according to my own abilities. It has taken me time to reach this realization, which is also fine. Every person has his or her own rhythm with which he or she reaches such acceptances.

And we have no choice but to respect that. A certain sadness blended with relief in my voice.

Right. There are those who will never reach that state of acceptance. There are people for whom it would take a lifetime, and others who will awake to it only in their last years on this earth.

We are each built differently. I discovered that, even about myself. It is impossible to speed up the process. There is a natural motion of realization, of transformation, of awareness, and of maturity. It is much like what happens to a fruit. It will ripen only in its due time. We are also like fruit. We ripen only when the time is right.

The problem is that we go on comparing our own rhythms with those of others, and we do it judgmentally—thinking that we are too slow, or too fast. However, there is no reason to make such comparisons, just as there is no reason to compare a bush to a flower, or to compare two different species of animals; to compare a lion with an ant, for example. The lion has the distinct qualities of a lion, while the ant has its own, completely different, distinct qualities. It is as if the lion would be passing judgment over the ant, and the ant would be judging the lion.

I definitely agreed with Shari. Sometimes, there are things I already know will happen; will be fulfilled. I even know I will be there, but I am still not there.

The guides of the Council of Six say:

"That you fail to accept your own rhythm, your attitude toward this gap—the space between where you are supposed to be and where you truly are—merely serves to make you smaller, makes you feel less successful, less accomplished. The place where you are now is exactly right for you at this current point in time. Remember this, dear people. What is right for tomorrow, will be tomorrow. Rhythm isn't a set thing; rhythm is always changing, fluctuating. You may be moving slowly now, and then begin to move quicker, or the opposite may apply. Accept this lovingly."

There is a gap, they tell us, between our mental under-standing and our emotional understanding. Our minds might understand, but our hearts have not yet reached the same realization. Often, there is a gap between reason and emotion. And before these two kinds of realizations become integrated, we cannot truly make a change, or truly accept change.

If, for example, I look at my acceptance of the world of channeling, my acceptance of being in that place, then I come to the realization that I have always actually been there. It has been a part of me even when I was a child, but I was then afraid. And, until I stopped being afraid, I could not truly be there.

This means that the pace of development, realization, is different from one person to the next, and it is not always pos-sible to hasten things, I thought. In other words, if I know how to recognize my own rhythm, I will be able to better accept the journey I am undertaking, and, thus, be better at understand-ing all things, because they all have to do with rhythm.

I asked Shari how a person can start to recognize their own rhythm.

Simply by paying better attention. Ask the questions—Am I doing things fast? Slow? Simultaneously? For example, even though I'm fast and focused on many things at the same time, it is still possible for the flow of my rhythm to be disrupted.

If, for example, during a meeting, someone is talking and someone else whispers something, this unhinges me. I lose my ability to listen. I have to stop and ask for quiet. If I am watching a movie and someone is texting and I see the light flickering from their screen, it really distracts me.

In the past it would have made me very angry; even cause me to be impolite from time to time. Today, though, I am no longer judgmental. If I feel I can ask the other person to stop, then I will, but if I feel that it is inappropriate, or unhelpful, then I won't. However, I understand that this has to do with me. That these bothersome things are disrupting my personal rhythm.

When I become aware of this—that this is my own sensitivity—I realize that whatever it is, it isn't an action that is directed against me. It is simply another person doing what is right for them. That allows me to feel less angry.

So, you are saying that rhythm has two parts? On one hand, there is the rhythm with which I do things; and on the other hand, there are things that divert me, disturbances, that are just as important to understand.

Correct. With me, for example, disturbances come at different levels. Not only is my particular rhythm slow in internalizing and understanding technology, it also disrupts my ability to focus; it creates a diversion that stops me.

Once you recognize both your natural rhythm and the things that disrupt it, and come to an understanding that they are both a part of who you are, you can find the correct path and act "better." When you recognize your own rhythm, you become less frustrated.

And I will tell you more than that. There is a rhythm to the soul—a rhythm for thoughts, a rhythm for emotions, and a rhythm for the physical body—and all these rhythms are different.

I laughed in agreement. So true!

For the physical body, it takes much longer. Sometimes you may already know something in your thoughts, in your spirit, or your soul; and you might even reach a state of emotional transformation, but the body is not yet there.

For example, I know, on every level, that we, as spiritual beings, have the strength to perform total inner healing. I have this realization. I have this thought, this emotion, but my body doesn't fully cooperate yet; parts do, others do not. I know, though, that it will eventually come. This will occur, either in my own lifespan or after it, but, for now, that world is still distant. It has a different rhythm, and my body isn't there yet. My body is still tired; exhausted. It invents different types of illnesses.

I'm jealous about that as well. I want to believe, but I still can't quite bring myself to do so.

This is fine. It has its own rhythm as well.

We shared an empathetic laugh.

I grew up in a home in which skepticism was a way of life. It was not a cynical skepticism, but one that was inquisitive. It came from a place that always doubts and never takes anything for granted.

This has many positive aspects, yes?

We held the sacred motto: What you see is what you get, rather than, what you want is what will be.

I was taught that, if you can feel it and touch it, it exists. If you can't, then it doesn't. But, later, down the road a way, I began to wonder. I began to see contradictions. I began to "know" things that were true even though they couldn't be seen.

When I was a child, I was afraid of being able to see beyond my physical eyesight. My parents looked down on this, significantly narrowing my sight until I finally blocked that ability entirely. It took most of my life to transform the rational perception—the fears, concerns and doubts—to finally realize that I have always been able to see "beyond."

So, I progressed slowly in this, stopping each time I felt this was it—this is as much as I can handle right now. In the beginning, for example, I was convinced that "energies" are just nonsense. Then I realized that everything is energy.

I can really relate to that. I grew up like that too. I also experienced a lot of inner resistance before each new development. There were voices that demanded of me, what if this isn't right? What if this isn't going to happen? Today, however, I am able to say to myself: Maybe such-and-such will happen, but you really don't know.

Just stay focused on the sense that you just don't know. This doesn't mean that something isn't true, it simply means that, at this point in time, you still don't know whether this is true. That is an entirely different concept.

My perspective is a little different. I know now that, to-day, before each new process of growth, there is a kind of struggle; a resistance, an experience, an inward and external reflection. I see it and I understand it, but it can make life very hard for me before this new process of growth is realized and accomplished.

I have a distinct knowledge that it is possible to experience growth simply, easily, pleasantly, and harmoniously, from within a sense of joy in all undertakings and in creation; without external triggers, without struggles, without any tests. Am I quite there yet? Yes. More and more so.

I have passed that stage of the struggle—the thing that comes to teach me to develop, to grow—albeit with lots of pain, suffering, and hardship. I chose the light. I chose the good. I chose the divine aspect within myself. I have grown, and I continue to grow all the time. I know that this is the direction in which all of humanity is headed, but humanity, as a whole, and the universe, as a whole, still has its own rhythm.

This brings me back to the subject of jealousy. Today, I am not as jealous as I used to be, but, hand-on-heart, I used to be jealous of people whose rhythm was quicker than mine; jealous of people who were able to negotiate their paths more easily or more quickly than I could.

Material possessions don't make me jealous. I have never been envious of people who have more than I. However, I was jealous of the paths other people have taken; of those who dared to express themselves sooner than I had.

Looking back, I note that there are many people who look at me and say, what a wonderful path she has walked, and what wonderful things she has achieved. Truly, I began to make progress only when I had said to myself, look only at yourself and respect your own rhythm. While I was busy with other people's rhythms and other people's paths, I was not being attentive to my own rhythm and my own truth, and I was unable to express myself in the way I am able to do today.

This may surprise you, but I, too, have felt that way. I wasn't jealous of the material possessions of others—I have enough of my own—but there are always those who have more. So, you can be envious of them. But that wasn't what was difficult for me.

I was jealous of spiritual teachers who have followers. True, there are the books I have written, and there is Essence of Life radio, but there existed a gap between how others perceived me and how I felt inside. I felt that what I was doing wasn't enough; which is human, which is a part of us.

Shari's words surprised me for a second. It had always seemed to me that there was something wrong about me because I was jealous of what other people were doing. Now, hearing that Shari had experienced similar feelings truly empowered me.

For a moment, that old voice, that had now almost vanished, spoke in my mind again. Who, exactly, can Shari Arison be jealous of? I felt ashamed for this brief moment of judgment, and then laughed in my heart.

This was a great example of personal rhythm. Getting to know Shari had slowly shattered the erroneous image I used to have of her. But, still, I occasionally found myself reverting to that old image.

It is important for me to hear this, and important that you say it. People do not talk about this enough. I used to be embarrassed by it, I used to try and hide those feelings. But the moment you put it on the table, you suddenly earn a great sense of relief. It is very human. It is simply what it is."

Right, but I think we put the things on the table when we learn to accept ourselves more. And, once we accept ourselves, we are able to talk about everything.

When we are discussing rhythm, we need to remember it is not just about our forward movement, but about an inward movement as well. For example, in a recent conversation I had with the Essence of Life employees about the will each of us has to grow and develop, one of the employees shared that she was about to give birth. "I'm very introverted," she explained. "While everyone is talking about growth and expansion, I feel I am actually in contraction."

I told her that she was in a process of growth as well, because contraction also brings growth. Nothing and no one ever stops. Our hearts keep beating. Our blood goes on flowing in and out of it. The waves of the sea come and go. All of nature is in a perpetual movement of contraction and expansion.

In the past, I viewed introversion as being negative, but with time, I came to realize that introversion is simply in my nature. I sometimes need peace and quiet; my "alone time." I have also come to realize that natural growth occurs in pulses; inside and out. Both are fine. Everything is a part of the natural motion and movement of things; everything is a part of the process of growth. It isn't as if I grow and expand one day and become introverted the next. Everything is a part of the natural movement we all experience.

As I listened, I thought about the many times I have been frightened and had "curled up" into myself.
In what way does introversion lead to growth?

You go "inside" so you can eventually emerge again with something new. We constantly undergo this cyclic motion. Once we understand the nature of this motion, we can stop judging ourselves for the introversion stage; stop feeling as though there is something wrong about it for which we must apologize. A realization is reached that there is something that is true for now that will change when the right moment presents itself.

Right now, I need peace and quiet. I cannot contain the external world. I need to go into myself right now, so that I will be filled with energy again. When you accept this cyclic motion, it stops feeling intimidating, and an inner peace is achieved.

I have never considered withdrawing into oneself to be a good thing.
Whenever I have felt that way, I would scold myself to get moving again. Honestly, it has never worked. It is as if something stopped me. I felt stuck.
Is withdrawal into oneself what causes people to feel stuck?

Yes. When people withdraw, it frightens them. It causes them to judge themselves. They think that something is wrong with them, or they're frustrated by the fact that, at that moment, they have no way of turning things around.

But, when we allow ourselves to experience this state of withdrawal and realize that everything will be released afterward, like the ebb and flow of the tide, then it simply becomes a natural part of life.

So, making progress always takes the form of such a "tango?" Even for successful people?
Shari smiled and continued.

It's like that for all of us; with everyone. If we understand this motion, we will stop being harsh with ourselves.

Why do we feel stuck? Because we misinterpret going within as being wrong. But, once we realize this as a part of the motions we must go through, that it is completely natural, we become familiar with our motions, and we learn to respect them. There are people who need more space and more time, while others need less. Each has their motional rhythm. It is a part of who we really are.

And that is actually a part of a person's rhythm?

Yes. We each have our unique fingerprint in that area, too.

I think we are used to referring to the subject of rhythm mainly in various actions, but there is also a rhythm to self-development, I repeated my earlier conclusions.

Yes, there is a rhythm to both, but consider how we look at people who don't do much; or, who do things very slowly. We say, what a lazy person, and see it as something negative. If we realize that this is built in, that it is simply their rhythm, we will have to ask ourselves whether or not we can accept it, and why.

I have my ups and downs, rhythm-wise. I can do a project at super-speed, but then I have to take a break.

I am also like that, but I think our rhythms are still fast-paced. Yes, we choose to take a moment, a timeout, but we also have the ability to do things quickly. There are those who don't have that ability.

There have been many times when I have been angry with myself over such "falls." I view them as falls, not as a break—not as a choice.

It isn't about ups and downs. It's more about going in and out. We turn in to ourselves internally. We process, move on to the next stage, and emerge again. It is a cyclic motion that is a part of nature. We humans are the only ones who feel guilty about having to take that inward moment.

My conversations with Shari made a lot of ideas and notions clearer to me. Her words sometimes offered a kind of assurance of things that I was already feeling.

That someone else who I appreciated and cherished, who had gone through a thing or two in her life, talked about the same things that concern me, made me feel I was not alone.

It wasn't like this only with me. Shari's words often exactly reflected things my guides had told me. It is important to speak about things, to share them with others, and then we are no longer alone with our feelings.

There is something nurturing and embracing about Shari, something that allows me to share my weaknesses with her. I assume the same qualities exist in me because Shari has shared similar experiences with me.

I again felt a sense of intimacy and I could not help but think of the past instances in my life when I had encountered a powerful, successful, or rich person, and simply assumed that they were self-assured and had no inner conflicts.

I smiled to myself. How easy it is for us to forget that we are human beings with feelings and fears who all go through hard deliberations. It doesn't matter how successful we are. It only matters how aware we are; how connected and attentive. That is what creates the differences among people; not external things like status, money, or financial success.

What is My Precise, Individual Sound?

We, each of us, without being aware of it, have a unique, individual sound that we transmit and receive. You receive my sound. I receive your sound. Some sounds are pleasant and soothing to me; others not so much.

The disturbances, the noises, just like those in frequencies and rhythm, obstruct our pure, precise, tuned sound. This is something we need to work on, because others will perceive whether my sound is "off" or is not in tune. In my previous books, I compared this to how an orchestra tunes its instruments before they play.

If we do not fine-tune our sound and are off-key, the person beside us will perceive this off-key sound, and not be able to see who we really are.

Sometimes we have an immediate aversion to someone we meet, even though they have done nothing unpleasant to us. We simply perceive their frequency—just as dogs can hear sounds outside the range of human hearing—and recognize something that disturbs us.

So, when I am precise with myself, my sound is also precise?

Yes. That does not mean we all have the same sound, though. Again, just like an orchestra, we each play our own individual instrument. In the same way that each musical instrument has its own sound and pitch, we each have a distinct sound. A violin has its sound that is different from a piano's, and different, again, from the way a cello or a trumpet sounds. Each sound is different. We each need to understand what our own sound is.

So, many times, what bothers us is that a person's sound is off, rather than there being a problem with the sound itself. We are unable to accept an instrument playing off-key. However, if the frequency is pure, we will be able to contain many more instruments.

Right. We all need to do our own fine-tuning. The more people in the world whose sounds are precise, the more harmony humanity will enjoy—just like in an orchestra.

So, I should tune myself twice; once to be adjusted to myself, and a second time to be adjusted for others, too.

Precisely. I referred to this at length in my previous books. When an orchestra plays, each musician has tuned their own instrument, refining their own sound, but they also respect the need for, and the place that the other sounds have. It is what creates music.

If you do not tune your instrument, or you do not listen to the other sounds, there is chaos, cacophony, and no harmony.

You can't tune someone else's instrument. We each need to tune our own instrument. The questions and exercises will help us tune ourselves to our most precise sound.

Is there someone around you who sounds harshly off-key to you? Where does it feel harshly off-key to you? Why is it disturbing?

If I know another person's instrument is off-key, will I be able to develop an empathy with that?

I suddenly realized that perhaps the people who irritate me actually have a personal sound that is out of tune. They are unable to express with precision what they think or feel. They come over as aggressive, full of blame, or judgmental.

That isn't because they don't care about me or that they don't respect me, it is simply because they have a difficulty. Maybe, if I remember that, I will understand that being off-key comes from a difficulty, not from indifference.

Yes. Instead of being taken aback, try to understand. That person has not yet reached their level of inner cleansing, their purification.

By tuning my own instrument, and by understanding how complicated it is to work on so many layers of the self, integrating and tuning them to a sound that is clean and purified, I can feel an empathy for those who have not yet managed to do that.

Sometimes there is a discordant sound to the things people say. I feel they are not precise and true to themselves, so what they are saying sounds out of place and is judgmental or hurtful.

I sank into thought and a brief silence fell between us until Shari continued.

Each of us has our own special shade of sounds that are like the different colors in the rainbow. While each shade is beautiful in itself, there are those with a gentler shade, and others with brighter colors.

We can ask ourselves, what shade of sound–color am I today? This can change from day to day. Sometimes you will get up in the morning feeling white, yellow, pink, or purple; sometimes you may feel gray, or even black. The shades change, but there is an essence—a shade that is your essence.

I thought about my own sound. Do I truly allow myself to voice it? Am I being attentive to it?

I remembered the words of the guides:

"An orchestra is formed by a group of musicians, each with a distinct sound, even if they are playing the same instrument.

"A good conductor allows each sound to be heard. The joining together of these sounds forms a harmony—the authentic voice of the greater music.

"You can also have an orchestra of voices. The conductor of this orchestra is the voice of reason, allowing each sound to express itself in turn. The conductor then decides which combination of voices to sound, to give expression to.

"The sound of your essence is composed of an orchestra of inner voices. When you ignore a certain voice, you lose a range of information that may help you.'

"Blocking some of your inner voices will make it hard for you to break boundaries, because they are related to your uniqueness.

"No voice is the voice of truth. Every voice brings something. Once you connect all of the voices, you will find the voice that is precise for you."

What Color Am I Today?

While each of us contains a whole spectrum of colors, we always have a color, or colors, that are dominant. These are the shades of our essence. With me, for example, these are the shades of yellow, like the sun—and purple, which for me is the shade of the consciousness. Indeed, many spiritual people who can see auras tell me that there is purple around me. Purple, in Hebrew, is considered a fine quality that is related to spirituality. It is the color that leads my way.

Why is it important to know what my shade of color is?

It is another part of becoming self-aware and familiar with your own self. We are not merely flesh and blood. We are far more than that.

Why am I drawn to a particular color? Why can't I tolerate another? Aren't all colors beautiful? Why are there colors one likes more, and others one likes less? Why are there people who wear only black? Why are there people who like wearing many colors?

You can learn much from knowing your personal shade and the meaning it has for you. You can learn much, both from what you are drawn to, and what you do not seem to like. It is an internal exploration. It is a part of who you really are.

I feel red. I have always felt red.
I thought about this many times, as part of my master's degree in art therapy, when I was asked to represent myself by choosing a particular color, it was always red. There were even times, having decided that, this time, I would choose another color, I still ended up being drawn to red.
Twenty years have passed, and I still feel that red is my dominant color.

Every color has its own significance, its own meaning. Red is the color of fire and passion, but it is also the color of anger. It has qualities. Every color has qualities.

So, if there is someone whose shade is bubblegum pink, which is a color I find less appealing, I might have a harder time connecting with that person?

Yes, but if you contain all possible shades in yourself, and learn to love all your different colors, you could also learn to love them all when they are found in others. Each of us is drawn to a particular color because it is our own shade.

Once you do internal work, once you have purified yourself, your spectrum of shades becomes wider. I can say that, these days, I love all the colors of the rainbow, but, once, there were colors I simply couldn't stand. In other words, there are colors that are aspects of myself that I have rejected. The moment I made peace with those aspects, I learned to love the colors they reflected.

Personally, red has been a difficult color for me throughout my life. I really couldn't stand red, and everyone knew it. In the many projects in which I have taken part, the people involved knew—no red!—never show me any red.

Then, one day, I came to the office wearing a red dress, and everyone nearly fainted in surprise. So, what happened? What happened was that I had learned to contain all the shades of myself.

I found myself picturing my various friends and family members, attempting to picture in my mind's eye the color in which I perceived them. Much to my surprise, colors did come into my mind. Sometimes it was obvious to me why the color I imagined them fitted perfectly the person I associated it with, and sometimes I really couldn't understand my choice.

So how do I know which quality a certain color has? What is the quality of green, for example?

The qualities are yours. You cannot generalize them to fit others. For me, green is the color of healing, but for someone else, green might represent . . . .

A hospital?

Exactly. For another person, green would have an uncomfortable association, and they won't like that color. There are books that interpret the meanings of various shades and colors, but I suggest you try to define them for yourself. What does each color mean for you? What association does it conjure up? It could be something from your childhood.

For one person, green is nature. If he or she likes nature, green will be a positive color. For another person, green represents a hospital. Hospitals promote negative thoughts.

If you have an aversion, you can explore it, learn to contain it, and you gain another shade inside yourself. You are then able to contain more of the shades of humanity.

If you can't contain a certain color, you won't be able to contain the person this color represents, and you will also be unable to contain a certain aspect of yourself.

This meant that if, in my mind, I saw my daughter in shades of purple, there would be no need to search the Internet for the objective meaning of purple.

She is purple to me. Individually. That is how I view the shade of her frequency. The better question to ask would be, what is purple to me?

An even more precise question to ask would be, what, in the way I perceive purple, represents my daughter? I see others in purple as well. A good friend, for example. However, she is not the same purple. My daughter's shade is deep purple, and my friend's is lilac–purple. The significance, for me, is different.

Purple connects with my will to heal people; to be more exact, to improve the quality of their lives. My daughter is studying psychology. My friend is an excellent parenting instructor who teaches parents to make peace and harmony in their homes. That is amazing, I thought to myself. Both work in therapy and caregiving. Perhaps purple represents treatment and therapy to me? Definitely food for thought.

Are there colors that are better or worse than others? Is white better than black?

No. There was a time I simply couldn't bring myself to wear black. I thought white was a purer, better color, but there is no such thing. It's like saying red is more right than blue. Or that blue is better than green, or green is more beautiful than purple. That purple is more important than pink.

Each is a different shade. You can't tell green that it needs to be red. All shades and colors are beautiful. You are red and I am purple. Which is more truthful? Which is better? Which is more beautiful? There is no such thing. You are unique, and so am I.

I thought about myself. When I feel myself to be the color red, I immediately become self-judgmental.

Perhaps I am fixated? Twenty years with the same color? Perhaps I am not allowing myself to change by blocking other colors inside me? Why red? There are plenty of other colors I like . . . . perhaps white would be purer?

And then I thought about the wonderful path I have walked over the past twenty years, covering a vast change in all of the areas I have dealt with. Yes, red truly speaks to me. Perhaps it is the color with which my soul came into this world? Maybe I should try to understand what it represents instead of judging it?

We use a sort of judgment? We try to see who is more powerful, or more beautiful?

But there is no such thing. It is simply different. That is why I find it strange when people tell me we are all equal. There is no such thing. There are equal opportunities, yes. This is something entirely different and very important, because we each deserve an equal opportunity, an equal voice, and equal rights, but we are not equal, not in the sense of being the same. One person will be tall, another short. Someone might be fat, another thin. Every person has their own uniqueness, their own shade and frequency.

I understood what Shari was talking about. Every single thing in the world has its own energy, human beings, too. This energy is called a frequency. Our frequency changes as our energy changes. It goes up and down according to our mood; according to our thoughts.

How do you recognize frequency in the context of color shade?

If you are in a dense frequency, a low frequency, shade has a black or brown color—muddy. One can move in mud, but the movement is slow and the mud sticks to you. You become a part of the mud.

That is often why the hard frequencies, like anger, cause us to become the anger, or the righteousness, or the bitterness, but a frequency that is airy, light, white, or even close to transparent, has a quality that allows you to move through it with nothing sticking to you. You are able to see the other colors, but they do not stick to you. You are able to move lightly and enjoy yourself. Airy colors have a higher frequency; a color that belongs to the spectrum of the yellows and pinks. They range from white to transparent

When we are in the higher colors we can see them well, and all the other colors, but when we are in the mud or the darker colors, we are unable to see that there are other colors?

We aren't able to see anything, because we identify with that shade, that frequency, so completely. It is like when a man walks into a swamp and sinks into the mud until he is completely covered. Mud is all he can see.

But a person with a higher frequency can also founder in the mud from time to time.

Of course. In my experience I can be moving as freely as if I were flying in the air when I meet someone in the mud. They extend a hand, or they embrace me, and I absorb that mud, because I as yet do not have the mental tools to remain on high. I fall right back into the mud. Suddenly there is sadness, and there is sorrow.

We need to understand that we influence each other all of the time, for good or for bad. This is why cleansing is so important. If I have a clear frequency, a light color, and a clean sound, that is the kind of influence that I exert on the world. When I embrace the world, that is the good I pass on.

On the other hand, someone who is moving in the mud, in the darkness, and struggling with negative and hard feelings, they pass it on and out into the world. It is only when we have firm inner foundations to lean on that these things cannot exert an influence on us.

Still, we are human beings who have our downs and suffer negative influences. However, the moment you recognize it, you will be able to understand that you are falling, because then, when you are in the mud, you know it.

When I am in the mud, all the harsh, difficult feelings rise to the surface, as if they have become more powerful there.

That is true, but that is not the case if you have risen up over enough time, and you have grown more powerful and empowered.

If your sound has become purer and your color airier and lighter, then, when you suffer a fall, you are aware of it and can mitigate its influence. You can see the light at the end of the tunnel. You know that this is temporary; that it will pass.

Our colors and shades keep changing. What is your color today? What is your frequency today? We each contain a full spectrum of all frequency ranges. We have moments when we are connected to a higher, faster frequency, and moments when we are connected to a frequency that is low and slow.

It's like the different sounds of a piano, from low to high, having heavier and lighter sounds. Once we learn to play all the sounds and move along the spectrum of the wavelength, we are able to contain all the colors and frequencies in the universe without passing judgment on them. First, though, let's get to know the complete spectrum of the wavelength; all of the different sounds, colors, and frequencies inside us.

We move along a sort of spectrum. Sometimes people who aren't spiritual experience a sort of illumination; some insight. When everything is flowing, going well, there is lots of energy, lots of productivity, and new things to experience. Then there become moments when you can hardly move. Nothing seems to be working for you. It's as if you are bumping into walls everywhere you go. Suddenly someone doesn't understand you and is angry, and then the refrigerator breaks down. Somehow, things just aren't flowing.

We all move on such a spectrum; sometimes we're up, and sometimes we're down. Sometimes we are full of energy, and sometimes we're drained. Sometimes we're happy, and sometimes we are very sad.

I thought about how our feelings influence our frequency. We call this our mood. Mood equals frequency. When we feel good, or when we are happy, our frequency is high, but if we meet someone who is sad, our frequency will become lower. We are influenced by frequency.

We are also influenced by external things: like the media, a book we have read, or a movie we have seen. Everything that affects us raises or lowers our frequency—sometimes in an instant.

This movement between frequencies can be very quick, right? I asked, sharing my thoughts with Shari.

Yes, because we influence each other. My frequency meets your frequency and resonates and influences. We can walk into a room with a great feeling, and suddenly we feel heavy, slow, stuck. We don't understand why. We have encountered heavy frequencies that have brought us down.

Sometimes, when different shades collide, there is no mutual attentiveness. At such a moment, it is better to stop, realizing that there is no ability to communicate, no genuine attentiveness, and no way to really hear each other.

In other words, if someone says, "he's not listening to me," then the accuser is not listening either?

That's right. It is mutual. They are reflections. It is better to stop and explain that we are different shades; that our perspectives are different. There is no right or wrong in this. This is your perspective; and that is mine. They are two different things. I see one side of the coin; you see the other. You speak from the side you can see, while I speak from the side I can see—there is no communication.

If I understand that we each have our own perspective, I can say, very well, I'll allow you to see my perspective, and you will allow me to understand your perspective. At that time it is important to know and say what sort of communication we are interested in pursuing.

I have decided that I am interested in constructive, unifying communication, communication that is empowering and nurturing. It does not matter with whom—in my relationships, with the children, with company executives, partners, in the community on Facebook, or on WhatsApp.

How did I realize that this was the kind of communication I am interested in? I have already experienced the type of communication that I am not interested in—those based on ego and emotions, anger and belittlement, blame and humiliation.

And, because I understand that this is not the way I want to be treated, I, therefore, do not want to treat others in that way. I need to declare to the universe what sort of communication I do want—and, that everything that is not in accord with that type of communication has to stop.

Today, when I realize that someone is making me furious, and my anger surges, I simply stop. At one time I would have shouted at that person. Today, I stop and say that I am too angry right now. I will talk once I have calmed down—period.

I say that from a place of choice. It is not the sort of communication I want. If there is belittlement in the communication, if continuing makes you feel small, you can simply stop and say, "I refuse to be belittled. Let's find a way to talk respectfully with each other, in an empowering way, and seek to build a bridge between us."

It is true that this is your responsibility not to take to heart, but if there is a communication, a conversation, you can reflect on what it does to you. Identify where you collide.

Let's think about people who are close to us and try to understand what color they are. Do this not from a judgmental place, but to try to understand where there are natural collisions that stem from the fact that there are differences between us. It will be easier to accept these differences; to accept the collisions.

When we say, "I expect to be understood," we are actually expecting to be accepted. Someone who sees things differently, from a different perspective, can't always accept my point of view.

Right. We need to think about the shade, the frequency, the sound, the rhythm. Even if we can't see it with our eyes, or hear it with our ears, something inside us does hear it. And see it.

There are sounds, frequencies, or colors that make us shrink; that scare us.

This is something we should take the time to observe. Usually, our immediate and instinctive response is to be defensive; to attack, judge, or blame, but, if we observe and understand that the person we are talking to is a color, is a frequency, is a sound—that irritates every nerve in our body—then we can try to understand why.

Maybe it's karma. Maybe that man had killed me in a previous incarnation, but, today, he is the nicest person.

Still, whenever I see him, a terrible and inexplicable fear wells up in me. Some things are far beyond the ordinary, and are much deeper than we can know.

That reminds me of how, in the past, I used to view assertive people as having attained success, even when they hadn't. I found them intimidating, and I sometimes had the need to belittle them because of my discomfort. It seems that when we feel weak, we have the urge to be right.

Correct, and then the other person feels the need to prove that they are right. But, as we have already said, each person is a color—red, or orange, or green. How do we take the good out of a person's shade, and the good out of another? After all, no one can change another's shade or color. And even if you disagree, you can still get to know each other and agree to disagree, because everyone is different and sees things differently.

How Do You Create Integration?

This book was written in several stages.

In the first stage, Shari and I simply recorded the conversations between us. When those conversations had been transcribed, I combined the segments, and, in the meetings that followed, we added elaboration, explanation, and clarification to those places we felt weren't clear enough.

Between our meetings, I spent time thinking about what we said. It was a great opportunity to look again at my life, my beliefs, my thoughts, and my actions. I sometimes felt great admiration in looking back at the path I have traveled, while at other times I felt like there was much more work to be done; that there are still places in me that are a little conflicted—that struggle with each other. I continue to judge these things and some aspects of myself.

How do you form a connection between all the parts? Between color, sound, and rhythm? I asked Shari.

It goes beyond connecting all the parts. To be fully whole, I needed to integrate all components of my essence as a soul who is living as a person upon the earth. In order to get to know who I really am, I need to get to know all my different components. It's just like knowing the various ingredients needed to bake a cake—flour, sugar, eggs. Then you can understand the whole.

This integration needs to be done on two levels; the human level and the soulful, or divine, level. The human level is composed of soul, mind, matter, and feeling. The feelings can be anger, insult, sorrow, sadness, or frustration. Whether it is joy, love, compassion, or even enjoyment, it is the complete spectrum.

If we refer to all of them as one, we can call them the "body of feelings," or the "body of the soul." They are a part of us as human beings. The physical body is a part of the human being. Thoughts are a part of us as human beings. It is a single plane. A single whole. A complete gamut.

Then there's the energetic side; the spirit, the soul. This is a never-ending plane—infinity, in fact. It is the divine spark inside us. It is necessary to achieve integration between the two.

What does that mean?

You have a human side and your soulful, divine side. You need to choose which of the two will lead the way, the divine or the human. Which of the two is going to manage me?

The human side is activated by emotions like anger, self-righteousness, destructiveness, and aggressiveness. There is also love and compassion, but, what manages us mostly, is the vulnerable, lowly, basic place.

The energy, on the other hand, is pure. It is divine. It knows only joy and happiness or love and unity. So, which will manage us? Yes, this sounds like an easy question to answer. Why wouldn't we want the divine body to manage and lead us?

In order to get to that level, we will have to go through a transformation to integrate the human body into this light. That is why we must get to know ourselves. We must become familiar with our feelings, our thoughts, the physical body and its energy, shades, frequencies, colors, and rhythms.

You cannot integrate what you don't know and don't understand. And, when we finally do know, and we do understand, we end up being "one"—a single, complete whole. Further, we, as individuals, need to decide which "one" is the one we want to be. What leads the way inside—into our selves.

So, the actual work one needs to do is the mental effort that involves self-awareness?

Yes, because it is only when we get to know ourselves, all of our various components, that we get to the stage where we need to thank them. We must thank our anger, because it has brought us this far. We thank insult, the feeling of abandonment, of being a victim, people-pleasing, all of these, because they have each taught us lessons. We need to thank the stomachaches, the headaches, and everything else in the physical body, because the body is the vessel that has brought us here. It is the vehicle in which we have traveled until today.

However, we can upgrade that vehicle; transform it, become familiar with its components, be thankful for them, and then choose to transform them into the light—into that place in us that is a divine spark that can grow from a small dot into a single, infinite, body of light.

That is our evolution and development—to reach the point at which we can become bodies of light. Some call it salvation, or the second coming. We can, each of us, name it anything that is right for us. It is a choice; to choose to make an exalted place in me, a pure place in me, the one that leads me.

If I have done the work of self-awareness, I then possess an in-depth knowledge of myself. I can now recognize when I have a troublesome thought, for example, or some feeling that makes me overly self-righteous—or guilty, or judgmental. I can stop to recognize these things, be thankful for them, and for my mission in this life, and go ahead to choose the divine spark within me and ask for the god inside me to be my guide.

So, this isn't a one-time process, like an illumination?

No. It is a developmental process. It progresses step by step. It is a transformation of one more part, one more aspect of us. At each point of choice I thank the human aspect, the one that normally controls us, and decide, instead, that the divine aspect will be the one to guide me.

My guides regularly point out that feeling as if you are "in the light" is the actual feeling of a connection with the divine spark.

"There is a lot of light in the world. We each have light in us. This light lives in us, side-by-side with darkness. The more you allow the light to expand inside you, the more the light will increase in the world. When you make the light more powerful, the darkness vanishes. Even the smallest light affects the darkness, but the darkness can never affect

the light. The more you focus on the light, the more of that light you will bring into your life.

"Darkness and light are perceived by you as good or bad; neither is so.

"There are fleeting material pleasures that are neither darkness nor light.

"Light is the state of being open to the divine spark, being open to your essence."

There are many times when I have experienced moments of light. It is a magical feeling of being connected to something vast and wonderful. And yet, even when I have been in that state, I continue to experience the occasional thoughts that take me back to the human aspect of myself.

So, the human aspect does not go away? Even when I am in the light? I half-asked, half-stated.

"No. So long as we are in our bodies, we are living the human aspect. There are those who choose to live only this way, only in their body. This is fine, but if someone has opened themselves and has gotten familiar with their spirit and soul, they can rise in the frequencies inside, rise in their perspective, and go on ascending to a higher place.

When you say "ascending," what is it, exactly, that you mean?

To rise and observe things from above; from a higher frequency. It is like drawing the numeral "6" on the floor. You look at it from one direction and see a "6." I see it from the opposite side and see a "9." We are both correct.

If, however, we rise up and look down from above, we realize together that it is both the numeral "6" and "9."

There is no right or wrong; these are simply different perspectives.

A lot is spoken about spiritual elevation, because, when you ascend, perspective grows. Our intentions change as well. We want to be good people. Our intentions are good. Elevation does not make us lose our humanity concerning love, compassion, and friendship, but the moment you rise in your frequency, and rise in your perspective, you realize that being defensive, or aggressive, argumentative, or insulting, is just part of the game that humans play while in the human body. We can choose to allow the divine to lead us and enable us to see this all from a higher perspective and to open our hearts. We develop, we advance, we return home, and this home is first and foremost inside us.

I thought how familiar I was with that concept. Many times, when I have been able to see things from a higher perspective, I have interpreted things in a completely different way. Sometimes, when something angers me, or it causes me stress, I am able to imagine looking at the situation from above. Doing this separates me from my emotions, allowing me to perceive things differently. The more I practice this, the more I am able to do it almost effortlessly. I wondered if it was the same with Shari.

And how has that process been for you? How do you do it today? What do you say to yourself?

This happened to me as I was having a conversation with a spiritual friend from Ireland who is a teacher and a channeler.

I told her that I have learned many methods and spent much time with many teachers. I have been channeling and gone through healing and initiation. I have spent forty years in deep spiritual processes. I have a professorship in the self-study of the consciousness, the spirit, the body and soul, and I have changed significantly. I have removed many layers, reached the core of the essence, and I have grown and matured. Still, I feel that something inside me is not yet completely solved—at least, not in the way I want it to be.

My spiritual friend said I should simply ask God to weave together my human and divine aspects. And, although I knew, even before she spoke, that this was what I should do, there was something about the simplistic way in which she said the words that allowed me to take it another step forward—to ask to form an integration between the two aspects, but with the divine aspect leading the way.

The moment I asked that, I realized that there are many things about the human aspect that no longer contribute anything. Battles are certainly not helpful, nor are the struggles or the resultant sadness and the pain. Yes, these have been important, and they have contributed over the course of many eons, but only because there has been no other choice. We needed them in order to survive and evolve, but we no longer need them.

I am thankful for what they contributed in the past, but no more. I now want to choose pure, clean, divine unification. That is what I want to lead the way with me, and in me.

And then, tier upon tier, divinity expands while the human aspect shrinks; one shrinks while the other expands. It is as if the basic, lowly, human aspect narrows, and the pure, divine aspect, that light-filled energy, expands, because there is more room.

When we first started our meetings, I felt that it was not even an option for me, the option to ask. I felt a pinch of jealousy, and I shared that with you, but once I heard you, I said to myself, what harm would there be to try?

I started asking the universe, the Creator. Honestly, I don't even know who I asked. I simply started asking. And, surprisingly, things happened. When I ask, I feel that I am able to focus my energy in a certain direction. That helped me to see things differently.

I want to add that some spiritual teachers say you need to stop asking and start demanding. I know some people cringe to hear that, while others feel comfortable with a demanding attitude.

There was a time when I started demanding things. It made me cringe some of the time, but I felt fine with it at other times. I think that each one of us needs to do this in the way most suitable individually. It is fine to ask; it is also fine to demand. What is important is your intent, and that intent is like a laser, it focuses you.

That reminds me of something very nice my guides told me. What is the difference between asking and praying?

The answer is that a prayer holds a much greater plea than simply asking for something. There is more intention. We do not pray for a nice day. We ask for a nice day. But, when there is a hardship, we increase our energy and we pray; praying has a greater intensity. It is the same with demanding. When I demand something, I put more energy and intent into it.

Everything is connected to where you come from. A prayer can come from a place of despair, or it can come from a very powerful place. For one person, it is a prayer, for another a request, and for a third it is a demand. But, yes, beneath all of that lies the clear intent of our will.

However, we also need to let go. But, we as human beings, find it difficult to let go of the outcome. However, with intent, demand, prayers, or requests, things come as they come, and proceed in their own way and arrive at the time they arrive.

It is necessary to let go of the expectations and the outcome. You need to ask and then let go. Demand and release. Pray and let go.

And believe that it will happen.

Believe and trust.

How Can You Let Go?

Many times in my life, people have advised me to let go. I have to honestly say that this has both angered and frustrated me.

How? How do you do that? How do you let go? If I had known how to let go of something that made me uncomfortable, or how to let go of a belief that no longer served me, I would have already done that!

I have learned many methods of letting go—of beliefs, of thoughts and fears—and the more I let go, the more things I still need to let go of. And, yes, I don't always manage to let it all go.

Shari had talked about how she had released a lot. I wondered what she had done—exactly—so I asked her.

I would love to hear about a time when you felt stuck but managed to free yourself.

It happens a lot, and in many aspects of life. After each significant decision, each significant action, there comes the moment after. It could be the moment after you have divorced, or moved to a new apartment, or a new city, sold a business, began a new business, or started a new job.

There is a period of time that can last a year, or even two, during which you continue to live your old life. It is a time when you haven't really adjusted to your new life. This is normally the stage when people feel stuck. For example, after I divorced, I decided that I wanted change in my life; change in my surroundings, in the sort of friends I had, and the way I spent my free time. The need for these changes was a part of the reason I wanted to divorce.

One's whole life can revolve around each decision. We feel stuck because we are no longer in our past, but we are not yet truly in our future. There is a moment in time when you are at a stage of incubation; a time between the past and the future stages. It is a place that people find very intimidating because it is a place of emptiness. It is a place of change, a place in which something new and unfamiliar to us is being concocted. It is the same in all circles of life, in all significant decisions.

When I think about being stuck, I think about situations in which I have an image in my head of where I need to be, but I am actually somewhere else entirely.

It's the same thing. In your head you are already in the new place, but you have not yet freed yourself of the old one. You are still in development, in the process of releasing the old and building the new. In your head, you are already in another place, but you have yet to fulfill the process.

You have the knowledge that you are able to expand; to grow and do things differently, to expand your circles. It is as if you have cast a net into the future, but have yet to reach the place into which it was been cast. Thus, you are no longer in the past. The past frustrates you, because it is no longer suitable to who you are, but you are yet to fulfill the new situation, which is why you feel stuck.

But you aren't truly stuck, you're evolving. It will pass. It's like an obstacle in your path. A mountain. Once you climb it, you will see the complete view. At some point you were stuck, but, actually, it is just one more stage on your path of personal development.

I thought about the guidance I had received from The Council of Six on this subject:

"Release is available to all. You only need to understand how it is done. When you think about something—are busy with it—you actually draw it toward you. Thought has a frequency. It has a magnetizing frequency. It is a physical law you are unable to resist. It is why, when you wish to release something, you must make your voice clear. You must understand exactly what you wish to release and why. The clearer the picture, the more regularly this will happen.

"And why do we say "picture," and not "thought?" It is because words can sometimes be unclear. Even when speaking to yourself, you may not fully understand what you truly mean. You may not be precise enough. But, when you are able to see the situation as a picture, the picture will always be precise. If it isn't precise, you will feel that, and need to replace it.

"A picture has an entirely different energy, which is why it is more significant. When you wish to release something, or to summon something, there has to be a picture. The picture has to be of a sort you fully understand, and be clear enough to realize what its subject is, and what your will in it is to be."

Indeed, it hasn't always been clear to me what I have wanted to release. The picture in my head was not clear and sharp enough. This happens to us all. We often feel stuck simply because we cannot see a different picture in our minds. We cannot think of a different way of doing things.

There is no point in trying to release something you are not yet ready to let go of. Sometimes your identity is connected to something only because you have grown used to it. When you try to release something from yourself, try to imagine how you will feel when it is no longer there. Pay attention to which feeling wells up in you.

Is it fear? Is it joy? This will answer the question of whether you have evolved enough to release it, or if there are more feelings and fears that you first need to cleanse.

What about people who feel they are stuck in situations they cannot get out of? Those who say, for example, I'm stuck in a bad marriage,

They are stuck in a bad marriage because they haven't yet reached a decision. For example, there will be those who say, "You just don't understand. I can't leave this marriage for financial reasons."

On the material level that is absolutely legitimate, but anyone who is able to break free of their boundaries, including financial boundaries, will find themselves in a better place.

It is important, of course, to examine each situation individually. Every person should check for themselves, because a person who does not feel at peace with their choice, feels divided and will be unable to reach a complete decision inside themselves; they will be unable to move. It is only when a person reaches a decision wholeheartedly that something will change. This isn't only about marriages. It is so for everything—for business, for work, for studying.

When we act from a divided place things go astray. That is why it is important to understand why we do not feel at peace with ourselves. This is the process of incubation I spoke about. There are those who will never be able to be at peace with themselves. It is why they will make no choices or, if they do, they will not act on them. For many people, remaining undecided is also a decision.

It is a painful decision, I said. I thought about similar painful decisions in my life, and my heart squeezed.

Not to cope is a choice. So is not to grow, or not to be nourished, a choice. Many times, people think they are stuck with no ability to move on, but we all have the responsibility and the ability to make the choice and create change; inside ourselves.

Change is not about getting a divorce, getting married, studying, buying a business, or going to work. Choice is, first and foremost, on the inside. It is what feels precise, and what makes me feel whole. When I'm whole, everything is good. That is so even if what I wanted didn't work out, did'nt happen.

When you make your choice from a wholehearted place, you experience the event differently—from a pure and whole place. If you do not make the choice wholeheartedly, and what we want does not come to fruition, then you begin to place blame; on yourself or on others. You feel anger, insult, and frustration.

I agreed with Shari. Everything happens on the inside first. As human beings having weaknesses and fears, we will always have decisions we will not be able to fulfill. How

many times have I decided to go on a diet? Or to not take
something to heart?
   How do you cope? Indeed, how have you coped in the past
with situations involving similar difficulties?

I have gone through a very long process, a very deep
and meaningful journey with this thing. I realized at a certain stage in my life that how I coped with things was not
the way I would have liked to have coped with them. As I
previously said about many of the things and subjects we
have discussed so far, I first knew what I wasn't.
   First, I saw that my thoughts were very negative. When
you think things won't be good, they never will be. Second, I had lots of fear and anxiety. I think this manifested
in my being outwardly judgmental of people and situations; full of blame. It took me some time to realize that
when we blame, we actually feel a great sense of guilt.

What do you mean?

Normally, we blame someone, or something else when
we are feeling guilty. We feel insecure, or helpless, or
frustrated, or that we don't know how to cope. It is much
easier for us to simply throw that burden onto someone,
or something else—that they did not understand me, did
not see me, did not hear me. It takes strength and courage
to look inside and say that it may be me; maybe it is I who
am not being understood. Maybe my communication is
faulty. Maybe this happens because I do not know how
to cope.
   I have gone through a process in which I have stopped
first looking externally to check who is to blame. I have
stopped being judgmental and getting into a whirlpool of

emotions, into a fight-or-flight state. I have worked for many years on the various parts in this array of the self; of myself.

It began with being able to identify negative thoughts, to see negative thoughts, to want positive thoughts instead; and then to understand how to get to those positive thoughts.

How do you recognize negative thoughts and move from them to positive thoughts?

We all know such thoughts. This won't succeed. It just won't work. People don't understand me. It's meaningless. It will always be like this. I will always be alone. I will never be understood. These are all negative thoughts that create a reality. If that is what you think, then that is what you have created.

It is easy to say I want positive thoughts. However, I do not believe that positive thinking comes on its own

It is first necessary to take a close look at our negative thoughts. Do not reject them, but embrace them. Understand where they come from, and then choose differently. It's really a mental workout—a gradual one, that slowly shifts from the negative to the positive.

I know this process from my own experience. Sometimes, even without noticing, I think to myself, this won't work. This will be too difficult. He'll never say yes. This immediately influences and lowers the energy.

It causes a sense of sadness in me, and sometimes anger or frustration, even before I do something. That is why it is so important to recognize these thoughts.

When I am aware of this happening, I am able to change my statement thinking. Even a small change can immediate-

ly lift my mood and my energy. For example, instead of this won't work, I have taught myself to say that I have a concern that this might not work. This turns the situation from hopelessness to one that is entirely possible, because I know it is only fear, and not necessarily the truth.
Was that what you did?

Yes. First, I began being aware of my thoughts. I began to literally observe them, like you would look at the words in a book. I observed the way in which I thought, the way my mind was working, my patterns. My mind had always been trapped in a loop.

I'm not being seen. I'm not being heard or understood. I am alone. I am miserable. I am lonely. Even when I experienced huge successes in business or when things were good with my children and with my friends, I was always in those places in my inner experience.

You cannot be happy like that. The things at which you are successful are never truly successful, and the good things never remain good, because if you think you're not being seen, then people truly cannot see you. If you think you are not heard, then people really cannot hear you. If you think you aren't understood, then no one will understand you.

I needed to see this, to see what I wanted. I needed to be seen, to be understood, to improve my communication with others.

Whenever I was in a conflict with someone, whenever I felt angry and full of blame, I stopped and asked myself whether this was doing me any good. Whether this sort of exchange, two people turning a deaf ear to each other, helped or advanced me?

If I put the emphasis on taking responsibility, then I will take that responsibility. I want to be understood. I want to be seen. I want to be listened to, so it is my responsibility to find the way for this to occur. I will try a certain way, and if it doesn't work, I'll simply try another. I will communicate that I want to reach a more constructive, more attentive discussion. I will turn the spotlight on that.

The same thing is true when it comes to feelings. I used to get offended easily and withdraw into myself. I would close up and feel sad and distressed. It was like a chain reaction. It could get so bad as to make me physically ill.

Once I became aware of this, I said to myself that I wanted to be healthy and calm. I want to expand my body rather than shrink it. Whenever I noticed myself shrinking and withdrawing into myself, I knowingly worked at expanding myself. Whenever I found myself being sad, I listened to the sad voice, embraced it, and I chose to be happy—to know what makes me happy.

There are aspects of ourselves that we need to see and observe. We need to see what we want to be different, and then train ourselves to ask for help from the universe, from God, and from inside ourselves, to make the change.

When there is a crisis, and you approach that crisis from a place of why has this happened to me? Why is this happening to me again? Why do I deserve this? You put yourself into a loop of victimizing yourself, and you feel miserable and full of blame. It is an energy that justifies itself.

We all go through crises. It is one of the things people don't understand. Life is life. It is the same for all of us. It doesn't matter who you are. It doesn't matter what you have. We all have beautiful things in life—marvelous, enchanting, happy things. And then we all have difficult, terrible things—crises and tragedies. What is the perspective we bring to those moments?

If I encounter each crisis with the realization and faith that everything I go through reaches to me to teach me—to empower me, expand me, serve me—then I am able to cope with each crisis in a different way.

The lessons of life are similar among all of us. We all encounter these loops. They repeat themselves not because of an external force or reason. Asking why I deserve this won't help. The loops keep recurring because I probably haven't understood the lesson they were trying to teach me. I probably have something more to learn.

Perhaps I need to release some karmas and reincarnations that are keeping me stuck in the same place. Perhaps I need to let go of restrictive thoughts and beliefs. If you look at each of your crises in this way, the picture changes.

Today, if I have a crisis with someone, I am thankful to them for being the messenger. I have reached a point where I have stopped blaming, and I have, instead, started blessing. I say thank you for the crisis, because it has arrived to help me release something, to open my eyes to something I haven't yet seen, so I can grow.

So everything, every behavior you encounter, has come to teach you something?

Of course. But it is hard. I have feelings. I have anger, frustrations, and helplessness. I can see my own self-victimization, my own misery, and the places where I have been hurt by someone and I am still aching. These feelings keep rising and surfacing. The question is whether I am to sink in these feelings and dwell on them or say that they represent my human aspect.

They will always be a part of me. I am a human being inside a body. I will listen to those feelings. I will embrace them. I will see what they have come to tell me. At the same time, I will look at the situation, or the person in front of me, and be thankful. Whatever it is, it is always to my advantage. It has come to help me grow, to release something in me, empower something in me. And then I can forgive. I can send that person the light, the appreciation, and see what I can learn from it.

There are small crises and huge crises. In the larger crises of my life the processes I have described have taken years. There has been a lot of pain, and a lot of vulnerability.

Unrequited love is a physical sensation that can actually cause death. It is gruelingly difficult and leaves a deep rift torn inside, but if I understand that that rift allows me to grow, to become more independent, to know who I am, to familiarize myself with myself, to understand what is right for me, to discover what I want, then I need to be thankful to the messenger who has broken my heart.

Actually, you are aided by the freedom of choice. Reality happens. The only question is how we choose to relate to it; how we choose to cope with it.

Reality happens to all of us. It isn't personal. If we look around and we open our eyes, we can see that everyone has to go through difficult things, challenging times. All of us. Even those who do not show it. Each person learns the lesson in their own circles of life and in the world. I am not saying this to belittle the difficulty of any crisis. It happens in the material, here on Earth. It is harsh, and it is painful, but things do not exist only on the material plane. We are both matter and spirit. On the spiritual level, the crisis comes to advance us, to teach us.

A recurring message I have received from my guides is:

"When we relay messages to human beings, we stress freedom of choice, but in many situations in life, when confronted with another person or a situation, you feel that it is what it is. Reality dictates a situation in which you have no freedom of choice at all. True, challenging, sad, and hurtful things may sometimes happen. You cannot always dismiss something that has happened, but you have many ways in which you can refer and relate to it. Sometimes what has happened is part of a lesson, of an experience your soul or another person had chosen.

"Remember that you can always choose how to cope with what happened—not by changing reality, but by approaching and viewing it differently, and then something in it might sometimes change too.

"When you feel weak and helpless, you put yourself in a fixated role. You then feel you do not have an alternative, that you do not have a choice.

"When a person believes they can act in several ways despite the situation being difficult or hurtful, they will normally act in a truer way toward themselves and toward others."

Experience has taught me that this advice isn't always easy to follow practically. In life, things happen to us that make it difficult for us to feel there is freedom of choice, but I know it exists in my choice of how I react; what I do after the fact.

As I thought about these things, I experienced a sense of discomfort once again. Many times, I have been unable to choose, even among the things I supposedly wanted to have a choice with. Perhaps I did not really want to make a choice?

I have often heard people say to others, maybe you just don't want it enough. This has always made me angry. I felt

*I wanted to, and just could not do it, and I always failed to
understand why.*

*This makes me think about the subject of weight, I said to
Shari, because I can tell myself that I need to choose—that
I need to want, but I just can't. Then I feel guilty over not
being able to want differently or to want enough.*

That is a good subject to demonstrate how this works. I
had experienced a long period during which I'd gained a
lot of weight and had not exercised. I am a very goal-ori-
ented person. When I decide on something, I do it—from
the idea, through the vision, to the enactment.

It's the same with my body. Sports, nutrition, diet, I
would come to a decision and carry out that decision, but
I would get tired. I would reach a point where I said to
myself that I wanted it to come from inside, not from outside; not because I had to do it, but because it was the right
thing to do.

It takes a lot of energy to undertake these things, and
I decided to completely let it go, to release it. Until that
came from inside me, I would do nothing. And what happened? I gained a lot of weight!

There were about four years during which I could
hardly bear to look into a mirror, or at my pictures. I just
couldn't stand the way I looked. I practiced saying to myself, you're beautiful, you're wonderful, you're charming,
but it didn't work. I didn't believe in myself. It was very
hard, but I had a goal. My goal was to let it come from
inside.

Every time feelings of guilt welled up in me, or I encountered difficulties, or even disgust, I reminded myself
that it was my choice. I reminded myself that I was able
to enter onto a diet and fitness regimen; that I had the de-

termination, and I had already done it in the past, but I did not want to do it from a place of regimen.

I wanted to do it from an inner and authentic place that came from the energy of vitality, from something internal that bubbled up from inside me. As long as it wasn't happening internally, I simply wouldn't do it. That was my decision. I began to bless my body, to be thankful for my body, that it should not be taken for granted that I had a body. I began to acknowledge my body.

I kept going back to my own authentic choice, and, finally, my body heard me. One day it came from within me. When it genuinely comes from inside, it becomes easy to carry out.

I thought about what the Council of Six says about inner thoughts and generating change:

"Your faith has a lot of power. When you believe that something is impossible for you, you will almost never be able to do it. You have been educated to use the term, "I do not believe" every time there is doubt, and whenever you do not know something. When you are unsure whether you will be successful, you say to yourselves, 'I do not believe I will succeed.' You block your own path, and you do not allow yourselves to be successful.

"We would like to challenge you to replace 'I do not believe' with 'I do not know.' I do not know does not necessarily mean it will happen. It may not happen, but, at the same time, you have allowed things an opportunity to happen. A person's faith has a lot of power.

"It is easy for you to not believe because you are afraid that if you do believe, hope will be created. If that hope remains unrealized, you will be disappointed. You are afraid to believe in what you are unsure will succeed, but it is hope

and belief that open the way. You are afraid to believe in your own abilities, because what would happen if you fail to realize them? It would be so disappointing!

"It is better to not believe, for then you may surprise yourselves. You actually create a more challenging path for yourselves. You are walking with chains binding your feet. You are walking against the current of natural energy. It is much simpler to want something without knowing whether you can achieve it. It does not block your path. It makes the path possible."

Since we started to write this book, I, too, have gone through a change in my eating habits. I decided to act while I was being attentive to what was truly right for me—and it worked!

How Do You
Build a Bridge?

It was a particularly hot morning. We were sitting, as usual, in Shari's office, sipping cold water. Somehow, our conversation had led us to a very significant subject, communication. We talked about family relationships, romantic relationships, and from there we went on to discuss relationships in general.

When communication is constructive, it is empowering, mediating; each side emerges from it with a good feeling. It is the kind of communication in which I listen to you, and you listen to me. I bring myself into it all the way, without fear, being fully authentic, without inhibitions, and without objections or resistance. My communication is accepted by the other side in the same manner, and there is mutual attentiveness, but that does not mean that we have to agree with each other. That is very important to understand.

What do you mean by saying that we don't have to agree with each other? I asked, even though I understood Shari's meaning. I wanted her to elaborate.

I'll give you an example. Not long ago, I drew something that looked to me like a field full of flowers. That was also how I felt when I drew it. In my mind's eye, I could literally see blue skies and light washing over the fields. I was filled with a magnificent sense of tranquility.

When I showed the painting to someone, he told me that he saw war in it; a storm brewing. I could have taken this interpretation personally and asked him how he could fail to have seen the real image I had drawn. Instead, I realized that my way of seeing the painting came from me; and that his way of seeing it came from him. I was able to agree to disagree, and to understand that he was simply coming from a different perspective.

When you are able to contain all of the shades and colors inside of you, because there are storms and battles in you as well, then you are able to understand the other person and why things are seen in a different way. I bring myself and the other person brings himself and we do not necessarily have to agree. I see one thing, he sees another. Our perspectives, the way we see things, are different.

I also think it is a matter of interpretation. There is no single way of seeing anything, but what helps you not to get angry or hurt?

If I go deep into my heart, and I reach a place of tranquility, of light, of unity, love, compassion, and good will, and the other person reaches that same place inside themselves, then a bridge is formed between us. If we try to bridge between ideologies, between different shades, concepts, or world views, that won't work. If you are connected to yourself, and to all the shades inside you, then the bridge is there, deep in your heart.

Because the way we see things is different for each of us, we can never come to an agreement, but, if we realize we do not have to agree, we do not need to decide on a single way, then we will be able to respect and see each other's path.

Actually, anger goes away when you don't try to reach a single way, but seek to make a connection.

Exactly. Instead of a solution, you seek a connection. I think that this would change the world. Connecting hearts.

When you open your heart, and contain first yourself, and then include others, you form the connections that will bring true unity. We do not necessarily have to agree.

Every person grows up differently, has a different perspective, a different history, a different education. What is true for me isn't necessarily true for you. That is fine, but if we continue arm wrestling, each trying to force the other's hand, debating who is right and who is wrong, then, as a nation, as humanity, as individuals, we will never be able to build bridges to connect us.

Because we were taught that there is only one true way, I thought about what my guides had to say on the subject:

"You always seek the truth, to find justice, but life is not an equation. Often, there is no single truth. Truth is a temporary energy, a thing that is true for a single person at a single moment in time. It also often happens that what you thought to be true is discovered to be untrue; and something you previously disagreed with is discovered to be true.

"When you realize that everyone is unique, it makes it easier to accept that each person sees things differently, thinks differently, interprets and understands things differently. So

*long as you are human beings, the differences between you
are a blessing and bring you an abundance of experiences
and learning, but they do not always lead to an agreement.*

*"Instead of seeking for a single truth, search for what is
right for you at a certain moment, and a path that is right for
you. That allows others to do that too."*

There is no single true way. There is, perhaps, a single
truth that is pure, clean energy—the light, but, so long as
we see things through the shells, it is impossible to see it.

The attempt to reach a single truth causes most communication today to be about that arm-wrestling, aggressive
style of communication. I will do everything in my power
to convince you, and you will do everything in your power
to convince me. That is not real listening; not acceptance.

If we are all different shades or different sounds, how
can we possibly completely agree with each other? But, if
we listen, and respect, and accept, and we find something
to bridge and connect us, we will both gain from it; not
because we have been able to convince each other, but
because we have been able to show each other a new perspective. That is the sort of communication I believe we
all must aspire to.

*Not to give up on yourself, but to conduct yourself from a
different place.*

Never give up on yourself. Ever! Instead, bring yourself in a way that respects not only you, but also others.
And do so not in a way that tramples, humiliates, or judg-
es the other. I bring myself, and I am willing to listen to
who you are and accept who you are. If we cannot come
to an agreement, let's learn the different angles, the differ-

ent shades, and all of the places that can be bridged. Let us aspire to find our common ground.

And what happens if the other side is being very aggressive, and you are unable to reach a constructive communication?

Then I let go. I release and I send lots of light, love, and good will, and hope that a constructive communication will bridge between us at some time in the future. You can't force it on someone else; it just doesn't work. I've stopped narrowing and diminishing myself—trying to please others, or changing myself for someone else's benefit. All I can do is bring myself to a communication with openness and love, show compassion to the other side, let go, and pray.

How familiar this sounded, I thought to myself. How many times have I tried to change things in myself because someone close did not like them.

This started with my mother and continued with romantic relationships and close friends. It never really worked fully in the long term. However, ultimately, the more sincere, genuine, and open I was, the more I brought my real self into the relationship, without change; in that way, the relationship became better.

It sounded as if Shari had experienced similar things. Did she, too, want the other side to accept her fully?

In the past, you used to minimize yourself, or you tried to change yourself. Why?

All my life. I was being a victim and a people-pleaser because I wanted to be loved. I didn't understand or see it back then. With time and self-teaching, I have learned to recognize this more and more, and I have had to let go of it, release it from myself.

What did you do when someone said something you dis-agreed with?

I kept silent.

You kept silent? I repeated, surprised.

Yes, I said nothing. I used the fight-or-flight method. Either I reduced myself, saying nothing, and withdrawing into myself (and drove myself crazy over it), or I set out on an all-out attack, with arguments and anger that followed.

In that way, you either belittle yourself, or you belittle the other person. Either you trample yourself, or you trample the other person. This is unhealthy, and it never leads to anything genuine.

In order for it to be real, we all need to be our real selves. There are people who have yet to reach that place. They do not wish to hear my truth, so they stomp on me and become aggressive.

Here we get into the subject of setting boundaries. I need to set a boundary and establish that I will not put up with being yelled at. I won't accept aggressiveness. If this is someone who isn't close to me, someone unimportant to me, I say goodbye to him or her. I finish the communication with love, with compassion, with the understanding that we have all come from the One, that we are all a part of God, that we each have our role and place in this life, but that that person does not necessarily need to be a part of mine.

If I want a mutual and respectful relationship, and someone does not respect me, then that simply isn't what I want. You have to know first what you want, and then you have to be that kind of person; first with yourself, and then with those around you. And, if the person with you cannot be respectful, or is incapable of being, respectful, you should feel compassion for them. If you have walked that path, and have come from that place, then you understand that there are those who are yet unable to see; those who are simply incapable of doing that as yet.

If it is someone close to me, a person I do not wish to see leave my life, I will have to set a different boundary. Perhaps I will have to part from them for a time, until they have done more work on themselves, and are wishing for a better, healthier relationship; one that is loving and pleasant.

If I realize that the person I wish to speak with is incapable of listening, incapable of seeing, incapable of understanding right now, I may choose not to speak. I will choose to be smart rather than be right. After all, if they are incapable of listening, what is the point in speaking? It won't do me any good.

You need to know what you want and what it will lead to. Will what you have to say lead to the outcome you want? Will it lead to a constructive communication and intimacy, or will it lead to an even worse conflict—an explosion?

So, we don't always have to say all we have to say, I declared. In my mind's eye, I could see the change I had gone through. In the past, whenever someone said anything, I always reacted immediately. Doing so fostered much tension, argument, and the feeling of unpleasantness. Over the years,

I have learned to respect the opinions of others, and I understand that I will not always be able to achieve a state of agreement, demonstrating that reacting is not always the wisest course of action.
Shari responded positively.

Right, but there is a difference between remaining silent from a small, narrowed, shriveled, frightened place, and remaining silent from a confident, powerful, present place; knowing yourself and knowing the other person, and choosing not to react because reacting at that moment is not the right thing to do, because it won't do any good.

Silence may appear on the surface to be the same reaction, but the two come from completely different places. When you do not react from a place that wishes to please, or from being a victim, from a place of belittling yourself, of being afraid, of feeling guilty and full of blame, then you feel horrible and it ultimately leads to nowhere and nothing.

But if you choose not to react from a knowing, tranquil, peaceful place that observes yourself, the other, and the situation, then you allow something else to happen. It may take an additional day. It may even take another year, but some development will ultimately take place, because an entirely different sort of energy is involved.

How Do You Dismantle Walls?

One of the things that typifies us are the inner walls we build around or inside us. We build them so that we do not get hurt, do not feel weak, and to (supposedly) protect and preserve ourselves. But, often, it is those very walls that prevent us from acting freely and reaching our goals in life.

If we have built walls around ourselves, we will have problems with communication and many other things, because we are unable to perceive. It is because anything that wants to get inside, to come through to us, will encounter a barrier.

How do you bring down a wall?

It's like peeling an onion, one layer after another. The barriers are what keep us stuck. We must explore and find out where they come from; their source, from which feelings, which thoughts, beliefs, or sensations.

What is the history of our wall? Does it come from our childhood? Was it a traumatic event we had experienced? Is it a reincarnation? A karma?

Sometimes, when a person faces a problem—the reality of an illness, for example, a severe or a chronic illness—they look only at the physical manifestation, not at the root of it. Its root can be many things.

Perhaps, as children, we experienced, or heard, or saw, someone with a severe illness. This got it into our minds, our set of beliefs, that everyone eventually gets sick. It turns into a self-fulfilling prophecy.

Perhaps it is karmic, perhaps the person had been sick in so many incarnations that they have come to their current incarnation to make a correction; to find a way of healing and to fulfill health. It may stem from a sense of insecurity or vulnerability and the illness has come to teach inner strength; how not to take things to heart, how to become empowered from within.

To get to the source, you need to peel layers away, like you would an onion—every thought, every belief, every feeling, every story.

We are full of stories. You need to find each story and release it. I have had many stories and many walls and barriers, beliefs that no longer suited me, and fears that were no longer a part of me."

Can you give an example?

In the past, I was a very vulnerable person, very sensitive. I viewed my sensitivity as a weakness, not as a gift. I was told that I was too sensitive, as if this was something negative. Vulnerability caused me anger and frustration It caused me to withdraw into myself. This caused me either to refrain, or to become aggressive. It caused many problems that have taken me long years to peel away.

Today, after all the peeling and reconstruction, I know I possess strength that is inherent in my sensitivity. That is a beautiful thing. I am sensitive to people. I sense people, I can offer a lot of love; a lot of compassion, attentiveness, and understanding, but I had to peel away everything that had been making that sensitivity manifest itself as weakness and hurt, as something that was keeping me stuck in life. I had to see it instead as something that advanced me.

I was also very eager to please. I lived in a sense of self-sacrifice until I realized I did not want to spend a lifetime trying to please others; that I wanted to live a life that was suitable for me—good for me. I did not want to be a victim.

This was an emotional confession that I was excited by.

A sense of great appreciation for Shari welled up in me. I thought about the beginning of our relationship. How easy it had then been for me to see her as someone who was beyond coping with regular human difficulties; as if, because of her great wealth, her life must be easy.

Now, suddenly, I could see, once more, how similar we were on so many levels. Shari didn't "make it" in life because everything came easy to her. She became successful in life because she refused to give up.

I find it very moving that you were able to succeed. That you were able to create such a meaningful, significant life's work, considering your vulnerability, your fears, your inclination to sacrifice yourself in everything. There must have been a very powerful, robust engine that propelled you onward. Even when you were much weaker, you had this strong urge to create.

My urge, my engine, has always been the true wish to carry out my mission in this world, but alongside it lived a very small ego that outwardly manifested itself in a very large ego. Often, what is projected as strength, can actually come from a sense of feeling very small. I wanted to show everyone that I could do things, and know, and see. This came from that small place, not from the larger one.

I was a child who felt she was never seen or noticed; never given her own place. I constantly felt very small on the inside, even as, on the outside, people viewed me as great. So, I had to prove to myself, and to the world, that this was possible.

There was a gap. My biggest frustration, throughout my life, has been the gap between my sense that I am small, weak, and vulnerable, and the realization of my abilities—of who I really am. I knew who I really was, but I was living my life from the opposite place; from a place that was very pleasing, very self-sacrificing—and lacking in confidence.

When you want to be seen and loved, but believe that you are not seen and not loved, that is exactly what turns out to happen. You achieve the opposite of what you want, because the energy you are transmitting is opposite. You need to melt this down, belief after belief, concept by concept, feeling by feeling.

It is a process that is repetitive and, even if we make the right decision and do the work, it may happen again, and we will fall back to those places where we want to please others and suffer self-victimization.

That makes us even more frustrated, because now we have the awareness, but this isn't enough. Once again, we find ourselves trying to please others, and, once again, we feel we are a victim. We once more suppress ourselves because we feel guilt and anger. We're angry with ourselves and angry with the world.

So it is necessary to melt down that anger, to be compassionate with ourselves, to dismantle the guilt, to give ourselves a hug, and to understand that it is all a process— one stage after another. There are no magic tricks. No hocus pocus. There's no such thing.

I've heard about people who have received "instant illumination," as though they were struck by lightning and instantly became another person. This may also sometimes happen to people who experience clinical death, see the light, and then, when they wake, find that something has changed in them. They are the rare exceptions, though. For most of us, it takes the process of life to advance, and its progress is step by step.

There are those who cannot understand why it is necessary to have to do so much work, which is also fine to feel, of course. If you are good, and your life is wonderful, and nothing bothers you, you are blessed. But, if you do not feel comfortable with yourself and your life, and you choose to blame and complain, remember that this is all in your hands.

I feel sorry for people who do not want to make the change, I said quietly, thinking about the many times when I had not dared to change. When I was unable to find the inner will to give me the power to change.

I think, in looking back at my life, it has been those places where I had dared to act that left the greatest mark on me. What is surprising is, even when I was unsuccessful with something, when I dared to act despite my fear, it nearly always made me feel good about myself, despite a lack of success.

Many times, your fear is bigger than your will, and you are unable to act to generate change. It is only when you stop to observe, that you gain the ability to change. When you stop and observe, that's when you can enhance the inner will by focusing on it. Then things happen.
It seemed as though Shari had heard my thoughts.

It takes real will to act. You cannot force someone to change or make a change. It has to come from inside them.

It is necessary to become familiar with the barrier, to understand what the wall is all about. Is it built of fear? Of vulnerability? Of a need for control? Or, is it habits, patterns, or false beliefs?

Different people have different reasons for building walls, and we need to check, each with themselves, what the barrier is made of and why you have built it. Through this will and recognition, it is possible to start releasing, dismantling the barrier, and constructing something else in its stead; an inner strength.

What do you mean by releasing and constructing something else? Was Shari speaking about the same process I had been thinking about? Perhaps she had taken a different path?

Releasing is, first of all, recognizing what is keeping you stuck, stranded; what is preventing you from moving forward. You have to have the realization that, if a wall surrounds you, it does not allow anyone to get inside, It is a sort of mask, and it does not allow you to progress because you keep running into a wall.

Once you recognize the existence of that wall, it is necessary to decide that you want to remove it and you understand exactly what it is about. You need to know what it is composed of. What are the things that prevent you from moving forward; that prevent you from growing and developing, that are not allowing you to develop an intimacy with someone else, that prevent you from accessing internal and external things.

For example, I may have built a barrier because I suffered separation anxiety in childhood and I do not want anyone to leave me ever again. Or, perhaps because I am very vulnerable, and every little thing insults and hurts me, I built a wall around me so that I would not be hurt."

You need to recognize what the wall is built of and start working with that value. If it is vulnerability, it means that I need to see that each time I am hurt and insulted, I also blame. He has hurt me. She has hurt me. He's the problem. She's the problem. I then realize that I am the one who is getting hurt and it is I who has the responsibility for that hurt.

I have built a wall so as not to get hurt, but this wall is obstructing me, stopping me. I need to let go of that vulnerability and, at the same time, build my inner strength. It is so necessary to simultaneously take down the wall and build strength in its place so I am not left with nothing, but, instead, empower the light in me more and more. This light shines outside of me. It serves as the boundary to keep me from getting hurt; not like a wall that seals, but like an energy expanding the consciousness.

However, it is important to remember that some of the walls were built to allow us to develop in a controlled way. Like in school. You go to elementary school, then middle school, then high school. You finish one stage, take the final exam, then move on to the next stage. It is exactly the same in the spiritual world. You go through stages. You learn, and then there is a sort of test.

You can call what separates the various stages a wall. We are tested, and if we successfully pass the exam, we receive things as a lesson. We learn from them. We develop in a positive, constructive, and empowering way. This does not come at the expense of someone else. We do not look outside, but inside. We develop, become empowered, the barrier is lifted, and we move on to the next stage.

There are those who would define this as a state of constantly being stuck. They are the people who will be frustrated by the fact that they need to constantly learn and be tested again and again, over and over. But the over and over may be the very test we must undergo to get to the next level, the next stage, the next development.

Is there a particular process you are thinking of? I asked, hoping to hear about a trick that always works—although I already knew there was no such thing.

No, because these processes are taking place all the time, at every moment of every day. There are small processes, little steps, but there are also big steps.

So, ultimately, you take down a big wall by taking lots of small steps?

Always. One step and then another. One stair and then the next. You can't jump from the first stair to the tenth. You can, perhaps, jump two stairs at a time, but you need to remember that you run the risk of falling. So, you ascend by constantly developing, by learning, step by step.

So we don't need to worry about the wall? If we go up the steps, stage by stage, we will ultimately scale it and move on?

Yes. Don't forget, we built these walls to protect our-selves, but as we go through the process, we no longer need them. We can take apart all those mechanisms, all those defenses. It is in our own hands. We have built these walls, and we are also able to dismantle them.

We must be aware of this, because people often think that what is keeping them stuck and preventing them from advancing is something external, but it always begins on the inside. If you are stuck externally, it means you are first stuck internally. Find out what the obstruction is. Find what it is that is stuck inside you, and when you are able to take it apart, you will advance externally as well.

Take our work on this book, as an example. We have had a lot to transform between us. In the two years we have been working on it, we have had to melt away the fears, the apprehensions, the judgment. On both sides. And, only then does the process allow for a much deeper discourse.

There has always been a good discourse, but occasion-ally barriers came up. I would say a certain word, and it would raise a barrier in you. Or, you would say something and a wall would rise in me.

Such a wall is a defense, a resistance. It emerged be-cause of our fear of being hurt, or it stemmed from an-ger, perhaps because we didn't understand each other and were insulted. These things are layers we had to peel away during the discourse between us.

I thought about our relationship and how it had changed since we first met. I'm sure you can sense this as you are reading this book.

Yes, there were also walls between us. Several, per-haps. Not because we wanted them, but because we are different and each of us brings a different set of values and beliefs.

Many times I told Shari that what connected us is this book, or some higher guidance, and, because we are different, without it our worlds would probably never have met. And now, despite all the differences, a deep and meaningful relationship has actually formed between us; a relationship that is unrelated to the writing of this book.

It has taken time. The connection and trust between us has been built step by step. I can see now that what bothered us were the beliefs I was raised on, which influenced the way I perceived Shari.

I think that one of the things I believed about myself when I was growing up, and one I got from my mother, was that I was a sort of monster, easily capable of hurting people, like a bull in a china shop. This concept made me raise walls, made me think I needed to be very careful with every word I said, because those on the other side might get hurt.

For my part, the first year and a half of working with you was accompanied by a lot of fear. A fear of being hurtful. I felt I had to protect you from me. I was always tense and nervous before and after each of our meetings. It was very important for me to do good; important for me that you would like what I do.

I think I wasn't really present in the beginning. And then, when we read the initial outcome of the book, we didn't like it. It was one-sided and not what we wanted. It was only when I started writing and adding my side, that I was genuinely able to bring myself into the relationship. Today, I feel completely connected. The shell, the wall, was something seemingly good on the surface, as if I were protecting you, but actually, it wasn't you I was protecting—it was myself.

Because I felt unwanted all my life. Because of the construct that told me I was never seen, never heard, and never understood, I experienced great difficulties. Frustration begat more frustration.

There was a wall. There was no heart-to-heart. In this process that we have gone through together, each of us has taken down our walls. Together, we have peeled away our defenses—yours and mine—until intimacy formed and an authentic conversation developed; a conversation more deep, meaningful, and moving.

Today I feel I have no more walls surrounding me—that I can say anything.

Me too, but it didn't start that way. And this isn't just an individual example involving just the two of us. This happens in everyone's meetings with others.

For most people, a meeting is about one wall meeting another, not a heart meeting a heart. In order to meet with someone heart-to-heart, you need to take down the walls. It is a process, a development. And that is what will bring the new world I envision.

Only now do I understand how much the stories I told myself, and the ones you told yourself, in the beginning did not remotely reflect reality. Each of us was in our own reality. It was not a pleasant feeling. It was exciting in the beginning, and there was a powerful sense of a connection from the first moment, but . . . .

. . . . but there was a good meeting, followed by a difficult one, and then it became uncomfortable, and then anger blossomed, followed by frustration—and then we both said we no longer even wanted to write this book at all!

That was a turning point.

Absolutely, because that was the moment that made me realize how important this book is. We have passed that barrier, and that allowed us to see the whole range—the scope of things—from the difficulties to the joys.

I wanted this relationship so much. I yearned so much for this book to see the light of day—so we could bring out a message—that I wasn't even present. At a certain stage, I just gave up. I said, "Enough, this is too uncomfortable, too challenging. Not everything has to be, and if it doesn't work, then I should just give it up." And the moment I gave it up, something else opened.

That is exactly what letting go is all about. The moment we let go—truly, genuinely let go—not ignore, not sweep under the carpet, but look at the wall to see it, observe what it is composed of, and let it go. Then something melts and fades, because we no longer hold on to it. When we hold on hard we prevent things from flowing. We prevent what should take place from taking place.

And, despite the fact that we never discussed it between us, we—you and I—went through the same process. Our energies influenced each other.

We shared a silence and then looked at each other with a great sense of relief. I saw an appreciation and a deep connection in her eyes, and I'm sure Shari saw the same in mine.

How Can We Recognize Our Authentic Will?

Change is one of the things that advances us most, although it sometimes makes that change harder on us, because it can create fear and a sense of uncertainty.

You say that the first stage in any process of change, connecting with yourself, of being who you really are, is about wanting to and actually recognizing your will. I was summing up Shari's approach, which matched my own.

Yes, but recognizing your true, authentic will can be very difficult.

Humans, these days, search externally instead of internally—a new car, a new house, money, career, relationships, children— the things that will make them happy and advance them. They fail to realize that nothing external can ever bring internal wholeness. We seek happiness rather than wholeness. This is a mistake.

However, it can't be helped. We are built like nature. We have both happiness and sadness in us. Sometimes we are extroverted; other times we are introverted. We have both black and white. We have everything in us.

Self-familiarity and precision bring internal peace. To be in a state of inner peace, you must live in peace with all of your various aspects and parts, not just the ones you like. There are parts of us we do not like. Sometimes we are angry. Sometimes we aren't nice. Sometimes we are nervous or stressed, and sometimes we are generous, happy, and full of compassion, friendship and joy. Internal peace means living in peace with all of our different parts.

And how do I emerge from this state and begin carrying out my own will?

First, you need to understand that the will has many aspects; many angles. People are used to thinking about will in the context of various actions—of work—but my body also has a will. My thoughts have a will. For example, I want positive thoughts, so, if I still have negative thoughts, I want to work on changing them, to shift them in a more positive direction. I want a healthy body. I want to feel pleasant within my body. My essence wants to be in a pleasant body.

There are many questions we need to ask ourselves in order to find out what our will is.

What is our physical, mental, and emotional will? What is our will for different actions? What is our vision? What have I fulfilled in my life? What haven't I fulfilled yet? What would I still like to fulfill? Is there a suitability between my will and my potential ability of fulfilling it? Is there a gap between the will and the reality?

I might want to be tall, but I'm short. Nothing will help that. If I want to sing, and I have a pretty voice, but I suffer from performance anxiety, that would be something I could work on. If, however, I don't have a pretty voice I would have nothing to work with, so I can redirect my effort and use my will to create something else. Understand that maybe my will is not about singing, but about expression.

We can ask ourselves where are the gaps between the will and fulfilling the will, and whether they are gaps we are able to change or diminish. There are things I can create and others that I simply can't. Do I know the difference between them?

I may want to be a good, generous, and kind person, but sometimes I'm not. Why?

I may, at any particular moment be impatient. Or I don't feel well. I do not have the physical, mental, or emotional ability to be nice right now. And that is because I feel uncomfortable. So, there is a gap in my will to be a nice person all the time, and my ability to be nice all the time. I feel the gap.

Another example: I am aware that I am, and all of us are, supposed to be a body of light, living our souls inside our bodies. That is my will, to live the God within me here on Earth. But what can one do? There's a gap. I'm not there yet. We are not there yet."

I agreed with her.

The guides of the Council of Six have many messages concerning the subject of will and generating change. I would like to share one of them with you. It is a message that I find to be relevant to this conversation.

"When you try to do something, even if it seems unrelated to other things, it probably influences your set of beliefs—your set of emotions. It influences who you are. It

is why, sometimes, even little things disrupt the peace and quiet.

"In nature, there is a significant rule. Everything needs to remain in a balance. When a body is motionless, it takes a vast amount of energy to put it into motion. It won't move unless it receives the right energy. The same is true for human beings.

"In order to start moving, to act in the way you would like to, you need an energy that is significant and right for you, one that will move you in the right direction, or you won't be successful. When you do not succeed because you do not act in the way that is right for you, then you immediately blame yourself for being weak, stuck, or for not being serious enough.

"Doing this, you not only isolate yourself from the strength you need to move, but you even intensify the force that is detaining or stopping you. This is why you feel stuck.

"When you want to do something, you must enhance your inner will. Think of what is drawing you forward. Think of what is stopping you. What must you take care of in order to move forward? That is a wonderful way of looking at things— logically, without being judgmental.

"So, the next time you want to do something and you feel you are treading water, remember that it is not really your fault. There are always opposing forces that stop you. There is will on the one hand; and doubt or fear on the other. Accept them with understanding. They are a part of you. You may be able to change them when you act correctly—when you understand the gap between your current condition and the condition that will allow you to move forward."

Shari spoke about this as well. I was curious to learn what she might suggest to resolve the gap within us.

How do you cope with the gap?

In the past, I wasn't able to cope with it at all. This frustrated me deeply.

I would talk and people simply didn't understand me. I wanted something to be done at work, for example, and there would be a wide gap between the vision and its realization. It would exhibit itself as a gap of time, a gap of abilities, or a gap of understanding. This drove me crazy.

I would also experience such gaps because I could see the potential in people; in the greatness they could have. It was very hard for me when people did not fulfill this greatness. I found it difficult to cope with the gap between what they were doing and the potential that was inherent in them.

It took me a lot of time to accept that such gaps have their reasons—and that the reasons were theirs. They had their own pace of doing things in their own time. I could never bridge those gaps for them. I could only make use of the opportunity to close the gaps I perceive between myself and the world — to work toward building a bridge. I understood that I needed to bridge those things both within and outside of me.

This began a process. Every time I recognized a gap, internal or external, I began to bridge it—very slowly, step by step. There are no rules for doing this, no guidebook. It is all up to the specific situation that has created the gap.

And, to bridge this gap you needed to identify and accept it?

Exactly. Recognizing and accepting it is very important.

If I want to run a marathon—and I've never run a mile in my life—then I need to bridge that gap. How would I bridge it? I get up on the first morning and run for five minutes. The next day I run for ten minutes; then half an hour; then an hour. Slowly, I will bridge the gap between my will to run a marathon and my ability to run a marathon—assuming that my will is achievable. The moment I recognize the will and I recognize the gap, I can bridge it. Bridging is a matter of doing.

Often I don't know whether I have the particular abilities needed. So, if I want something, I start bridging and see where it takes me.

But it is also very important to accept the fact that sometimes the gap is between your will and your ability.

One of my sons loves to give speeches and is a great speaker on the stage. A while ago, I mentioned to him how jealous I was that it came so naturally to him. Yes, I do have that ability. When I get up on a stage, I speak excellently, and that is what comes across, but, emotionally, it is always difficult for me because I'm naturally shy and very sensitive, aside from other reasons.

I had tried to bridge that gap for years before I reached a certain point when I had to accept that this is simply who I am. There are times I feel uncomfortable about giving a public speech, and other times when I feel more secure and relaxed, but I now put my emotional abilities into the times when I feel comfortable.

Actually, you acted without preliminary judgment. You went on stage to speak again and again, and encountered emotional difficulty every time. You were successful with your actions. You then stopped and observed, and were able to recognize that you are capable of speaking, but, perhaps, you weren't interested; perhaps the emotional toll was sim-

ply too great. This, however, did not come from a judgmental attitude—whether you are capable or incapable of giving public speeches. That wasn't the question.

True. Because maybe I wanted something and it just was not right for me? Or maybe I didn't really want it? Maybe I wasn't precise enough with myself about my will?

A large part of bridging gaps has to do with self-familiarity and self-awareness. Between the will and the realization there are many variables.

I may say I am interested in a relationship, but if I do not take into account that I am afraid of relationships— because I have been burned before—then I will fail to see what leads me; what isn't my will, but my fear. Until I realize this and let it go, I won't have a relationship. Wanting something isn't enough. We must understand ourselves and our will and whether we want to advance and develop.

Sometimes we are afraid to want, or we want something that isn't suitable for us.

As a baby grows, their will appears to be natural; to always be right. Then they begin to observe reactions from the world around them. The baby is taught that wanting certain things might be wrong. Sometimes they may want things that aren't comfortable for society. Many times, a baby is threatened or even punished. And, in this way, we learn not to believe in our own will. We are taught to believe that sometimes our will may lead us to a painful place; that sometimes the will can actually be harmful.

The child, who, in an outburst of creativity, scribbles on the kindergarten wall is scolded by the teacher, and, lat-

er, is reprimanded and punished by his mother. He or she simply wanted to express themselves. The child does not always understand that their will was good and it was proper. It was just the realization that was wrong. The lesson that child has actually learned is that their own will is dangerous; that they cannot trust or believe in it. This happens to many of us.

And so, as adults, we act without being attentive to our wills because the will might sometimes seem frightening and make us feel insecure. When a place is unsafe, the meaning is danger; we might get hurt, or we might hurt others. It is important to remember that the will is always right. It is always genuine and true. It is only the way it is realized that may sometimes be wrong, or unsuitable.

Normally, when a person wants something, acts accordingly, and achieves an undesired result, they assume that the will was wrong. That is an erroneous assumption. The way was wrong, not the will. The will always exists. The moment we recognize what our true will is, that is the moment we take the first step toward realizing it.

Sometimes I want something, but there is confusion about it, which is why it is important to understand not just what I want, but why I want it.

What is the force that propels us to want things?

There are two types of forces that propel us.

There is the old force—the one that propels the whole of humanity. I feel I am no longer propelled by that force. It is a force that stems from anger, resistance, aggressiveness, self-righteousness, or vindictiveness—emotions that give us an energy; that push us forward. It is a force that comes from the residue of the past, from negativity. You could call it oil.

Then there is the new force. Let's call it solar energy. It is a force of light, or regenerating energy. It is more refined; softer, purer. It is the force we wish to transition to.

However, once we make the transition, there will be a period of emptiness, of an empty space. We release one propelling force, the one that comes from the ego, from the will to show, to prove something, because we understand that if there is anger involved, then we deal with it, and realize that there is no such thing as self-righteousness because we each have a different perspective. We realize that there is no room for being vindictive, because we are not in a place of light and essence, and we can see that we are all one.

So, once we have released this residue, the "oil," what actually propels us? What drives us forward? For a moment you no longer have the old force, but you do not yet know how to use the new force.

Today, I am at a place where I understand that what propels me is growth, development, creativity; a will to create and a will to influence. I have no urge to prove anything nor to boast about anything. I know what I need to make things more pleasant for me—better, purer, more precise—and that is what propels me. I operate on an energy of light, which is far more energy efficient.

What do you mean by more energy efficient?

Think about it like an old car. It gets worn out, rusty, so it consumes more fuel. Humans are the same. There is wear and tear and illnesses and fatigue. The new force is much quicker, lighter, more precise, so it takes far less of it to get you farther. It moves and nurtures you from a very different source.

What about the sense of mission? Many people who come to me feel that what propels them, what is pushing them forward, is a will to do good in the world; to make a difference.

I, too, have always felt that I act out of a will to do good. In retrospect, I see that I have truly acted out of a sense of mission, but there was a lot of ego involved in that as well; people-pleasing, and a need to prove something to myself. I also wanted to do good because things weren't good for me. It is very selfish when you want a better world because you need to make things better for yourself.

The place I am at now is that I want a better world because I want a better world. Period. It is not because things aren't good for me personally, or because I can't cope with the world outside myself and want to change it so it will better suit me.

Shari's words aroused a resistance in me. If I act to do good, what difference does it make what my motivations are?

If I'm not feeling good about myself and I want to do good to make it better for myself, as well as for others, what would be so bad about that?

There's nothing bad about it. It has nothing to do with good or bad. I have done this for many years, and I believe that I have brought a lot of good into the world over the course of those years, but I came to this mission from a sad childhood—from harsh feelings and from an inability to cope with evil and unfairness. Today I come from a different place, a place where I feel good about myself.

I am using a different energy. I see the world from a higher perspective. I recognize an awareness that there is a reason for everything. That is the game here on Earth. Humanity learns from it. My mission is to do good, to bring light, to help others transition into the new propelling force, while bringing this from a place of abundance, not from a place of scarcity.

Shari was painting an idyllic image. A situation without judgment. I am not there yet. I'm not even sure I ever will be. I think that so long as I am human, I will have fears and feelings. The question is, to what degree do they propel and motivate me.

I feel that, in many things, the old force still motivates me. Fear motivates me; my own survival motivates me. And yet, I have already released things like vindictiveness, anger, and accusation. Even if I act out of those feelings sometimes, I can see what I am doing and I can work on it. So, I feel I am in an entirely mixed place.

How do you reach the void? How do you connect with the new force?

I was able to reach the void only when I realized that the old force wasn't what I wanted. But I still didn't know how to act from a different place.

I'm the sort of person who likes precision. I was a perfectionist and I was hard on myself and the world. That was my driving force, but when I realized I did not want those difficulties, that I wanted ease, that I wanted to be propelled from a better inner place, a place of awareness, a place of growth, that was when I was able to reach the void.

I realized what wasn't right for me, but I still did not know how to accumulate the right forces—how to harness those inner forces to propel me forward. I could already see it, sense it, understand it, but it still wasn't a force that could move me. The moment I declared to the universe that I wanted my own good and the good of others to be as one, that I wanted balance and harmony, the moment I let go, it happened. Just like magic.

When Shari spoke, I felt a new doubt.
Was it realistic to act only out of the positive energy, the "new energy," as Shari called it? I then realized I was being judgmental again. Perhaps it was possible! Why block the opportunity? I felt my doubt and resistance fading, and I was ready to continue listening to the way Shari had acted.
And what happens when you start acting by using the new force?

If I ever wanted the process to end—if ever, it always tired me—the work, the development—then, today, with the new force driving me, I have come to the realization that the process will never end. And! I am able to see the beauty in it. It is like a flower with eternally opening petals; more and more so. With creation that never ceases, it is a joy.

I won't tell you that ego doesn't raise its head from time to time. If I receive compliments, I see how the ego enjoys them. I then have to tell myself to choose. I do not deny the ego. We each have ego. Sometimes that ego is high; sometimes it is low.

Today, if I see the ego rising to the surface to have its fun, or rising to receive a blow—it doesn't matter which, it is the same thing—I am able to thank it and make my choice out of humility. It is my choice.

The ego will emerge from time to time. I might catch it or I might not. It is a part of me. But the awareness leads to choices, and the choices lead to further awareness.

I feel that when people act toward me motivated by the power of the old force, it creates aggressiveness. My reaction is much less pleasant than when people approach me softly. Softness generates love in me. Aggressiveness automatically raises my own aggression.

It was like that with me as well, from the time I was a girl until a few years ago. I have always viewed my sensitivity as being a disadvantage. I always knew I was very vulnerable. If I was insulted, I shriveled and closed myself up, or I went to war. Aggressiveness would draw aggressiveness from me, because it was something unresolved in me.

When aggressiveness is resolved inside you someone can approach you with an aggressive attitude and you are able to reply with softness because you have been there. You know. You understand, and it no longer intimidates you. I won't tell you that it's pleasant. It is much more pleasant to have love and softness in your interactions.

But, when your own aggressiveness is resolved, you are in a place from which you are able to return a lot more love, and it is also easier to establish boundaries. You can see from that resolved place within you, that the person facing you has still to reach that place of accepting love; they do not want to, they are not ready, and they cannot see.

So, you establish a boundary, and you say I don't want to allow this into my personal space. And then, like I said, I send an energy of love, and I pray that only good will happen to that person. I do not return ill will with ill will.

And how can this realization guide me in my life? Can it help me be more precise with my inner engine? Can it help me replace the old force with the new one?

I can't tell how it might guide you or any other person. I am merely sharing what I have learned, what I have experienced, and where it has led me. For some, it will ignite the spark of realization. For others, it will help a little, and for still others it might help a lot—or not at all. There are those who will even find it irritating. That is no longer my responsibility. I bring myself and my truth into the world. It will touch each person where it is supposed to touch him or her. It will be different with each and every one because we each have a different structure of personality, different thoughts, different beliefs.

How will someone use it? Take it? That is no longer my business. Each of us is responsible for what we do with what we perceive and what we choose to accept. I wish only that what I have to say will help and bring goodness to others.

I'll admit I expected some sort of guidance or explanation, and perhaps I'm even surprised that you have not provided one. However, I also think that sometimes one of the most useful things to do is not to give explanations or guidance. I agree with what you say, that each should take this to their own place. It will open what needs opening—if that person allows it.

How to Let Go of Expectations and Judgment?

I very much enjoyed our conversations.

We were sitting in Shari's office, as usual, when I excitedly shared with her the news that my new book was about to be published. With apprehension there is also excitement. Each new published book is like a birth for me. I have no idea how it will be received nor how it will influence others.

I shared these thoughts with Shari and said that I hoped my expectations would be fulfilled and that my book would touch the hearts of people (in the same way I hope this book will touch yours). I'm sure we all have expectations and are afraid of disappointment.

You have mentioned our expectations. This is a subject I have been thinking about quite a lot, because of a channeling message I received on August 8, 2019. It appeared simple enough on the surface: Be at peace, my child, without any expectations. It was said to me over and over again. I could not understand what was expected of me, and not knowing caused me stress.

I tried to understand what I was supposed to have no expectation for, and immediately thought that something bad was about to happen. I had to calm myself and go deeper inside myself and observe. I noticed that in almost every situation in which I have high expectations of my-self—to be nice, to be connected, to be happy, to be full of energy. And, whenever I am tired, not being nice or angry, I am disappointed with myself.

Our expectations of a person cements our perspective of them—for good or bad. If someone is charming, there is an expectation that they will always be charming. Then, if they are having a bad day, and are a little less than nice, we are very disappointed in them—in the same way we expect someone who isn't nice to never be nice to us.

We peg them, and do not allow ourselves to see anything else; to see, perhaps, that the person has changed. Maybe they have softened and opened their heart. We also have expectations generated by certain situations.

I attend an event, for example, and because it is being held in a home that belongs to people I love very much, I expect it to be fun, but I'm not having fun. Or I go for a trip somewhere I like, but it's too hot, or the schedule is too tight. We also stick our perspectives on situations, and then there is a gap, because everything changes at every moment. And that is why it is important to, first of all, free yourself of expectations.

How do you do that?

As always, we must be aware of what we expect and how much we expect it. I wasn't aware of the expectations I had. I was amazed to discover the extent to which

I wasn't aware of their intensity and sheer weight of the expectations I had had. And when I did observe this, I realized that I have expectations at any given moment, with every single thing, about every person, in every situation. Again, as we already said, when you observe and realize it, you can start changing it.

Another thing I was able to take from the channeling message was in its first part—be at peace —to be at peace, in silent tranquility, in focus. If I have a certain will or intent, and I am at peace, perfectly balanced, I will be able to release it to the universe. In other words, I do not base my expectation on the outcome.

The fact that I want something in a certain way, that I have good intentions, or that I send a certain address to the universe, is fine, because we are creating a reality with our thoughts. But what does that look like? What will the result be? When will it happen? Those are all things we need to let go of.

Yes, I thought to myself. Letting go of my expectations regarding the book would be the right thing to do. And so would allowing the universe to take me to the place most suitable for me.

I often think I know what is right for me and expect a certain thing, but something else happens—and, sometimes, that something else is much better. What Shari says is that sometimes our expectations ruin things for us because they cause us to miss other opportunities that come across our path. Something else might happen that would be to our advantage, and when you are stuck, you prevent yourself from enjoying those opportunities.

So, each expectation becomes cemented. It causes me to be stuck and causes others to be stuck as well.

Yes. And it cements the situation, too. I saw this in the last election campaign here in Israel, which was very charged. I heard many people ask, what difference does it make? Everything will stay the same anyway.

That is an attitude that causes us to be stuck. The expectation that there will be no change cements the lack of change. It doesn't matter what the outcome is, because, really, the outcome is out of our hands. Only the intent and the choice of which energy we project are in our hands. We need to release it; to let it go.

A lot of people don't want to have expectations because they are afraid of disappointment. To me, this seems as though they are mixing up expectation and hope. And those aren't the same, right?

Right. I can hope. I can wish for something, but at the same time, I can release the expectation and the outcome.

What is the difference between expectation and hope?

Okay, let's say I really want and hope to find a spouse. That is one thing. But if I expect a relationship and it doesn't come, that is something else. That is being in a state of constant disappointment. I won't be able to enjoy anything else that is going on in my life. Amazing, wonderful things may be happening to me, but if they are unrelated to a romantic relationship, I will be in a state of constant disappointment. It will paint my whole life in dark colors of disappointment.

So, this doesn't mean I don't hope to have a spouse. It doesn't mean I don't want to have a spouse. I do. I want a relationship, and I hope to have one, but how can

I expect it? After all, I don't know where this will come from. I don't know who it will be. So I need to let go. I should not hold on to the expectation. Holding on will keep me stuck.

You can remain hopeful, because hope is good. It's natural, but expectation means you keep waiting for something to happen. Then, everything becomes about waiting. There's no movement.

Right. Expectation also causes us to search for something that will prove that the direction we thought about is true; proof from someone, from the universe, from yourself. That also becomes something that is stuck. It stresses and disappoints you.

Our intentions can create a reality, but how exactly that creation will come, and when, that is beyond our control. We need to release our urge for control. It isn't simple, but if there is enough will and enough intent, and if we keep being aware, we might be successful in this process of releasing.

Awareness is very important. It was only when that channeling message fully registered in my mind that I was able to start being consciously aware about my expectations. It really surprised me. After all, I had been working on my awareness, my consciousness, for forty years, and now here was something so simple, yet so powerful and significant.

I looked at Shari and smiled. Self-development is something that never ceases, and it has great value. To me, each new discovery, each insight, each point of view that hadn't been there before, brings me closer to myself, and there is

nothing more exciting. It is a wonderful thing when I do not find myself judging the path I am marching on.
And what do you think about judgment?

I think that being judgmental is having expectations that are combined with being critical. In other words, I expect something from someone. I am stuck with that expectation and that is the image I have. And when what I expect doesn't happen, or when something else, different from what I expected, happens, judgment follows.

Judgment causes a lot of separation because it makes us take a dim, intolerant, unaccepting view of others. It begins with self-judgment. We constantly judge ourselves. I'm not tall enough, not thin enough, not nice enough, not smart enough. I am unsuccessful, unfulfilled. I'm a failure. There was a time when I used to judge myself even for being tired; disappointed in myself.

I tried to look at why it was so difficult for me to accept being tired. This judgment harms us, because it raises helplessness, frustration, and anger. It is the exact opposite of self-acceptance and love. Being judgmental means that you constantly feel something is wrong. If we do this to ourselves and we do this to others, how can we expect a whole nation, a whole country, humanity in its entirety, to act without being judgmental? We judge each other for good or bad. If someone agrees with us, we judge them favorably, but if another person has a different color, a different view, a different perspective in opposition to what we think, we judge them unfavorably.

True, I thought to myself. Once again, I remembered a message from the guides. They say that the things that rob us of the most energy are anger, judgment, and criticism.

These expend energy on both sides. Supposedly, people pass judgment and criticism on others in order to help them, but a person who views the world through judgmental eyes views himself with the same judgmental attitude. That lowers the energy level. Judgment distances good feelings. While we criticize others or ourselves, we are unable to feel love.

A person at the height of their power does not observe the world through judgmental and critical eyes. So, if being judgmental is harmful for us, why do most of us so often act that way? What causes us to judge others, and, mainly, ourselves?

Perhaps it is the fear of making mistakes? I decided to ask Shari what she thought.

Do you think it is because of fear?

I think it is because it is hard for us to recognize different shades. Each of us thinks we know best, and each of us thinks we want the best, and each of us thinks our motives are the best, but even good people often make the mistake of judging others instead of understanding others.

Get to know others. Accept others. And, thereby, put judgment aside.

Judgment isn't observation. I can observe something, get to know someone, and come to the realization that they are inappropriate to who I am, or to my life. But I do not negate, I do not judge whether that person is better or worse than me. They simply are not suitable for me.

If, say, I am a liberal, non-religious woman, and I am faced with a piously religious, ultra-Orthodox man, for example, I can see, observe, accept, and understand that that is his shade, and that he would not fit into my life, because I wouldn't be able to have him as my guest, and because he wouldn't even look at me. But I will not judge him. That is his way. That is his shade, his belief, his perspective. I can respect it, but I can also see that he isn't right for my own life and that I am not right for his life. That is different from judgment.

Right. It doesn't assign a score to it; it doesn't rank it.

Exactly. It is like a jigsaw puzzle of a landscape. There is an area of sky and an area of land. Each of us connects to one's place. If I am in an area of the sun and someone else is in the area of the forest, that is neither good nor bad—they are simply different areas, but, together, they form a single image.

Interesting, I thought. Why does Shari think that judgment is harmful?
In what way is judgment harmful to us?

It causes separation. Aggressiveness. Self-righteousness.

During one of my channeling sessions, Beyon said that we always compare ourselves only to those who we believe to be better, more gifted, and more accomplished than ourselves. When we judge ourselves, it is never positively.
We almost never say I'm better. Normally, we look at someone else and say that he is doing it better than I am. We do not compare the sum total of our traits or actions to those of others, but only one trait or a single action— and always harshly. That is why Beyon says that judgment makes you feel worthless.

There is much truth in that, but there is an opposite side to this, as well.

There are those who are vain and arrogant. They think, because they have a higher education, this makes them wise and intelligent, while others remain stupid. A lot of that judgment may come from jealousy, or from the need for control. There are lots of reasons, but, ultimately, if we want to love ourselves, to love others, and to achieve harmony in the world, we must release that judgment.

I don't claim this is an easy thing to do. We all judge. Me, too. If someone speaks to me unkindly, that makes me very judgmental. I get hurt. I am reduced, but, because I am in a state of awareness, I will be able to look inside and see what this reflects in me, what is happening in me, and why it has upset me so.

My first reaction, however, will always be judgmental. Who does he think he is? That initial natural reaction involves judging the other person. Those who are not in a state of self-awareness remain stuck in judgment. This is their problem. It's their fault. But when you are in a state of self-awareness, you can let go of judgment and start doing internal work.

There are those who say that, unless we are constantly judgmental with ourselves, we will never develop. They claim that this is the only way we can ever improve; see what we can get better at.

I think that this is one of the most misguided opinions it is possible to have, because judgment is always to our disadvantage. Passing judgment isn't objective observation. It is why it will always rob us of our strength and will never allow us to be at our best.

It is the difference between judging and observing. Observing is about examining the situation and seeing it both ways; both in relation to myself and in relation to others. That is essential.

Being judgmental is about something else, about forcing things into a pattern and marking them with a score. It causes blame, guilt, and fear. If you are judging someone who is belligerent, for example, then you are afraid of it. Judgment creates many feelings: insult, frustration, feeling small, demising, and, on the other hand, arrogance, or a feeling of worthlessness. Judgment makes no contribution. It is only when we move on to observation that a process can begin. So long as we are in judgment, we are stuck.

That is a problem we have with communication. We create a story about someone, or about a situation and people believe that story and start talking about it—which gives it more power. We become stuck in our judgment toward that person and turn the story into a reality.

An observation is like looking at a painting without saying something like this red is too bright, or this green is too light. You simply look at the painting.

Right. When I wrote my first book, *Birth: When the Spiritual and The Material Come Together,* someone in my office read the manuscript before it was published and suggested to me that perhaps I needed to change this, and perhaps I needed to change that. I replied that he was cutting my book to pieces. After all, I had written it out of my very soul. If it had been a painting, would he have told me that the reds should be changed to blue, and green would be better off being purple?

That is the painting I created. You like it? Wonderful. You don't like it? Wonderful. But it is my painting. The same is true for the book. It is my book. You may connect to it, or you may not. You may love it, or you may not. Both are fine.

In order to transcend beyond judgment, you need to transcend the gravity. To rise up, you need to first shed the extra weight, the layers. When someone is deep in judgment, in criticism, in self-righteousness, in blame, and has a wall surrounding them, it is very difficult to transcend.

We need to start a process of shedding. To simply shed everything keeps us stuck. Everything that holds us to the ground and cements us like concrete, we need to let go of. Once we do the processional work, shed the shells, layer after layer, we make ourselves lighter, and then there is a point from which we can start transcending and observing things differently.

The moment we transcend, we rise beyond gravity. We realize we are all one, all connected. The illusion of separation, the me-versus-you, and the self-righteousness, criticism, and judgment are all a game of gravity.

When a person walks down the street, they see only themselves. If we go up to the hundredth floor of one of the buildings to look down at the street, we will see a lot of people, shops, the windows of the other buildings, more streets, cars, trashcans. From above, we see a much larger picture. We see that we are a part of it. And then there is nothing to judge.

How does judgment prevent us from being who we really are?

If I am judging myself, feeling I am not good enough, not tall enough, not capable enough, then I am angry at myself, because I wanted to do something and couldn't. I leave myself in a reduced state.

We are very complicated. We are comprised of many moods, changes, and situations; we are being influenced and we influence in turn. If we allow the flow to be what it is, we will see that sometimes we're small and sometimes we feel tall. Sometimes we will feel beautiful, and sometimes ugly. Sometimes I feel brilliant, and sometimes I feel stupid. Sometimes I am successful, and sometimes I fail. The moment we let go of judgment and understand that we constantly flow, we allow ourselves to be who we are at any given moment.

I thought about us, about how we often want to get to a certain place in life, and it seems we would be happy if only we could get there. Then we do get there and feel happy because of it. But, slowly, as time goes by, we get used to it and stop being so thrilled and happy with our accomplishment.

Suddenly, it seems to us that there is yet another point. If only we get to this new point, we will be truly happy. We are being constantly judgmental of the path we are taking, with the place we have reached, and with our accomplishments.

If we could anchor ourselves in a good place and that would be enough, so be it, but even when we get to the good place we have been striving to reach, it fails to make us feel good over time.

Yes, but nature keeps changing and so do we. If we are stuck, then even if the images around us change, we won't be able to see it. We are so convinced that this is simply the way it is, that even if something else stands right in front of our eyes, we won't see it. We do not allow ourselves to truly see or hear, because we are stuck on something. Our essence is constantly flowing. Our essence has many different shades. We need to allow this. We need to allow this motion. Allow the changing. Allow all the shades to be present inside us.

You are talking about our opinions and our beliefs. They have all been stuck on something. Most of us are stuck on who we are. I am like this. I am not like that.
When we compare ourselves to others, we compare the image we have of ourselves with the image we have of them. That, as we have determined, makes us weaker.

We each compare ourselves to others. I do too, but that isn't right because we are unique and singular. One of a kind. Each with a unique fingerprint. There are no two people in the world with the same fingerprint.

No two people have the same soul. We all come into the world with uniqueness. So, why do we always try to compare? To define? Why do we need to do that?
I suddenly felt angry at this phenomenon of comparing ourselves to others and being judgmental. We are exposed to it at a young age and it accompanies and burdens us throughout our lives.

"It supposedly gives us confidence, but is an illusion.
Think about the days when people were hung or burned in the city square. How was it possible to live with this, to tolerate it? If we are judgmental and we justify our judgment, that will give us the confidence to do anything. It is the same in our times. Perhaps not in the city square, but maybe in a newspaper article, or with gossip, making it essentially the same. It can kill the soul.
It is much more comfortable to be judgmental—much easier. To be loving and accepting is difficult. It involves

work. It involves taking things apart layer by layer and asking questions and going down a long path. Judgment gives people the feeling that they know what is right.

And there are many times we do this to ourselves.

Right. We put ourselves down. Perhaps not in every area or in every single thing, but we do kill parts of ourselves. That is why self-acceptance of all the various parts in us, and self-love, free of judgment, are so important. It is unconditional love that accepts all the shades, inside and outside, but that does not mean it is not necessary to put boundaries in place.

Boundaries are very important. However, that does not mean that I now have to accept every person, even if they have done something inappropriate to me, or something I disagree with. I can accept that it is their story, the will of their soul, but that does not mean I will allow it to happen in my own life. I can accept it on the level of the soul, because maybe that person has come to teach me something, or to correct something in this game that is constantly being played on Earth, but that does not mean that, on the human level, I will allow it to enter my life. Rules and boundaries are needed, but on the soul level, I will accept it as a part of the game.

So, my understanding has to begin with myself. If I am able to see and accept the parts in me that I find difficult, then I will be able to see and accept those parts in others. Acceptance is not about love.

Accept yourself. Love yourself.

Her words irritated me a little. I keep hearing the platitude, accept yourself for who you are. I don't find it easy to accept everything about myself.

Let's suppose I have ADHD. I would like for it to go away, but still I live at peace with it. I accept it.

I think you should take it a step further and love the ADHD. Love yourself with the ADHD.

That is hard for me. I can love myself with the ADHD, but to love the ADHD itself. . . . ?

Why not? It's a part of you. It is who you are. I, too, have ADHD. I used to be ashamed of it. Today, I've learned to love it. It is who I am. I can want to improve. I can find ways to learn, but I need to accept the present situation at this present time and love myself. The moment I accept and love myself, I can also make changes, but, until you love all the different parts and aspects of yourself, they will keep on colliding and conflicting among themselves. There will be no inner peace.

Something inside told me that she was right. I wanted to ask her how to do this, but the voice inside me said go slowly—step by step. And, the first step is to not judge it. Once we stop fighting a certain aspect of ourselves, it stops angering us. Then, over time, we are able to accept it as a part of us.

What is the Evolution of Humanity?

Many of the people I meet treat reality with an it-is-what-it-is attitude. Some also treat others with a they-will-never-change attitude. Actually, we are in a perpetual, constant process of change—we human beings and the universe in its entirety.

I asked Shari for her thoughts on the subject.

People tend to think that if something is a certain way right now, then it will remain the same forever. That is surprising, because the world is constantly changing. Why, then, do people fixate the situation and think it will always remain the same? That simply isn't going to happen. So, always leave the option for change open.

If a situation is undesirable and painful, it doesn't mean things will always stay that way. You can declare what you want to the universe, and then let go. Whatever needs to happen, will happen.

But even if we don't want to change, refuse to change, we will ultimately change. It is impossible not to. We change all the time. We are first fetuses, then babies, children, teenagers, adults, old, and then we die. We are in a process of constant change in our bodies.

Humanity changes too. We are not the same as we were a hundred years ago, and we aren't yet what we will become a hundred years from now. Evolution takes place whether we actively participate in it or we don't.

There is something much larger than ourselves. Still, we have the opportunity to be a part of creation in our consciousness, to initiate who we want to be, and how we want to be in the greater picture. It is in our hands, and we can be proactive in the collective process of development. If each of us is proactive, growth will take place accordingly.

Because each of us is affected by others, and affects others in turn.

Yes. Humanity's development is collective, but it is also dependent on individuals—what each of us contributes to the general picture.

Think about how you see yourself ten years from now or how you see the world a hundred years from now. Imagine, dream. However, how do you see yourself, and how would you have liked to see yourself? Those are two completely different questions.

You may think that ten years from now you will be in the same place, but where would you like to be? Dream. Go for it. If you go for the dream, what will actually stop you from achieving it? Your thoughts? Your power of creation? You can play with that too.

It is only our thinking that stops us?

Individual and collective thinking, yes.

There are things about collective thinking that can keep us stuck at a point having no critical mass of will or intent, or belief. This is demonstrated in many processes in humanity's history—slavery, women's rights, whatever. With everything that developed there was a certain consciousness, but until that consciousness developed to a critical mass, it could not be fulfilled. We have personal powers of creation, yes, but we also have a collective power.

When I was fifteen, Disney World opened in Orlando. I remember a ride called Tomorrowland. I sat in my seat as it moved through different family scenes—how the world looked then, and how it would look in the future. The highlight involved seeing someone sitting in front of a computer, talking to someone else in a different place. That technology did not exist then. It was in the realm of science fiction, but someone had thought about and imagined it, and, although it took years, the world is there now. Long ago, people dreamed of flying. Today, anyone who can afford to, can fly. It is becoming more and more accessible.

The moment things like cars and telephones were created and became accessible, we no longer think about how different this made things. It takes only one person to make a change, yet it is the mass of humanity that dictates those kinds of changes. It becomes easier and easier to create a different future. Anyone can do it.

What do you mean by saying that anyone can change the future much more easily?

Today, it is much easier to change the future, because the spiritual consciousness has risen and there is much more awareness—self-awareness and collective-aware-ness. Technology has connected everyone. In the horse-and-buggy days, it was hard to know what was happening on the other side of the earth. There was a collective con-sciousness, but there was no awareness. And everything was very slow.

Today, there is a collective consciousness as well as awareness, and, thus, the possibility of creating a collec-tive connection through different technologies. Generat-ing change is much easier. Someone writes online that they want to start a protest movement and, suddenly, there are millions all over the world who join in.

Look at Greta Thunberg. She motivates teenagers all over the world to take action for climate change mit-igation. That is something that would not have been possible to do in the past. The moment it exists in the consciousness, and in people's actions, it also exists in its realization.

It is much easier today, but the question remains, will we choose a better future or a worse future? We have the ability to create peace, but we also have the ability to cre-ate war. So, which do we want to choose? Everyone will say they want peace, but do we really use our spiritual consciousness—our words and our actions—to promote it?

The collective consciousness is always a little behind the consciousness of individuals. A shift in the collective con-sciousness takes more time.

It also takes time in the consciousness of individuals. We still have a way to go to reach the place where the material and the spiritual connect. We are yet to fully assimilate that; yet to fully realize it in a physical, material way. So, how can one expect collective implementation? It will happen only when there are more and more people bridging between heaven and Earth, between the spiritual and the material, between peace and war, between separateness and unity, between density and light. Only when there is a critical mass of people who have made this personal transformation will the collective transformation happen. That is why it is so important for each of us to do work with ourselves, because the work and the changes each individual achieves, is done both for themselves and for the whole world.

Can you give me an example of the collective consciousness today?

You can see our collective consciousness in terms of money. We put power in the hands of those who have money, material possessions. Whether we look at those who have money with sympathy and admiration, or we look at them with hate and repulsion, it is our contemporary collective consciousness. Money is power, and power is important, so we need a lot of money to have a lot of power.

But the meaning of life is much deeper than that. It involves reaching the essence and the God within me here on Earth; as individuals and as a collective.

I'm not talking about religion, I'm talking about light, about love, about compassion, and about unity. That is the essence of our existence. Our collective consciousness is still not there. It is in a place that diverts us from the essence.

Why do we appreciate someone who is famous and rich more than we do a teacher who dedicates an entire life to educating others, or to a doctor who works to save lives around the clock? Why do we, as a collective, direct the spotlight at material and superficial things instead of at things that are more meaningful and significant? It is a matter of a collective consciousness, and it is a potential we fulfill as a collective. We have a lot of different potentials, and we can change that.

It was interesting to hear Shari talk about this. In a material world, there is a lot of room for material possessions—for money—but far too much significance is placed on it in the collective consciousness.
What do you mean by potential? I asked.

Potential is a crossroads. It is a possibility. It is a choice. To give you an example, I am currently at a crossroads in my various business endeavors. I can continue investing, or I may decide to stop investing and dedicate all my time to being an artist. We all have many different potentials. We can choose our future, while in the past it used to be more anchored and cemented.

What changed?

Earlier, we were led. You were born, you went to school, you got a university degree, got married, had children, had a career, grew old, and died. There wasn't a choice because we were not in a state of awareness.

Today, everything is open. We see this in the material world because the Internet shows us the endless possibilities. This has been made possible because awareness has risen, opened, and everyone can choose the future they want.

That doesn't mean that life does not still come with its challenges and struggles. We have those every minute of every day, and we need to stop each time to make decisions about our choices—about how we choose to conduct ourselves when we are faced with what the world brings us, but we are able to make a choice. That is the main thing. We can choose what we want and how we want to live.

I thought about what the guides say about the current age. Today, we are truly no longer being led. This can lead to confusion sometimes, because some of us were not raised that way.

In the past, much emphasis was placed on development and growth. Industrialization, scientific, technological, and medical progress have all advanced rapidly in the past century, and the price this progress has demanded from the individual is that they put themselves at the service of the collective for the general good.

The collective was the most important thing. In Israel, for example, a country had to be built. Individuals were needed to dry the swamps. People lived in poverty and difficult living conditions without feeling poor and miserable because they did it for a greater purpose. These things happened in other places, too; in Europe, for example, and during the Great Depression in America. These are things that the whole of the Western world has experienced. A hundred years ago, the Western world was still focused on survival and the collective had to harness the individual.

Consequently, social rules evolved regarding what a person should believe and what they should think, in order for society to develop. There was no room for individuality, for the desire to stand out. Leadership was all about the greater good. There was no room for individual expression.

The previous generation did what had to be done. They had to provide. They had to work and start a family. There were a lot of things they "had to do."

A person who did what they had to do felt fine. Most people had no ambition to develop and find themselves, but only to do what was expected of them. They were to act in the same way their parents and their parents' parents did before them. Women raised children, and, if they worked at all, to help support their families. It was usually part time, or at jobs considered suitable for mothers.

This was also reflected in the set of values that dominated society. These were qualified as the greater good, modesty, humility, settling for less, being a part of the group, and other such. Beliefs allowing one to settle for less were adopted because there was simply not much to be had. In this present age, conditions have changed, and have even turned upside down.

Today, society is led by individuals who constantly put forth ideas. The people who propel the development of now are individuals. Society encourages ideas, inventiveness, and vision. This is an age in which humanity is encouraged to develop. There is no longer a social dictate that tells us what is right or wrong. Everything is permitted, so long as it doesn't harm others.

There is much potential for material abundance, and an abundance of possibilities and opportunities. We can do anything. There are a lot of talented people who learn and do things, but in looking at the general contentment of the population—the general sense of self-fulfillment—it is noticed that there is more frustration, and a lot more difficulty. This abundance of opportunities contributes to people get-

*ting lost—exactly why listening to your inner self, being con-
nected with your inner truth, is so important today.*

Hearing you compare the past with the present makes
me realize that I view this concept in a different way. In
my view, it wasn't a situation in which the individual
worked for the greater good, but a situation in which the
individual sacrificed themselves for the greater good.

The woman sacrificed herself for the sake of her husband and children, and the husband sacrificed himself to
provide for his family. Sacrifice is very different from an
awareness of unity.

True, people are far more individualistic today, but I
believe it is a part of evolution. In order to truly be for
the greater good, for unity, we each need to be in our own
essence and our own individual uniqueness. Such a state
can be reached only when we know ourselves and put the
emphasis on ourselves. It becomes possible then to be a
part of the whole without sacrificing yourself—to be present with all your power.

What is Your Vision?

The abundance of opportunities and roles is confusing, causing people to focus on external things such as profession, status, and material possessions, and less on their essence.

I think we have gotten used to living with masks on our faces in this world, indulging in roleplaying games, and we have forgotten who we really are. I remind you of the example I gave you earlier of the stage actor getting up on the stage. Every day, he portrays a character from a Shakespeare play, but when he gets home, he is a husband, a father, or an uncle. Imagine what would happen if he forgot to go "off character" and continued to play a Shakespearean figure in his own house! We have become such characters. We have forgotten who we really are.

How does that hurt us? Why should we try to change that?

Because it is the reason for all the sickness, and all the insanities, and all the battles! We have drifted so far from our essence, that we have forgotten who we are. To heal ourselves and our world, we must first come home to the authentic internal self of who we really are, and understand that the definitions we have are simply roles we play in this current incarnation; mother, father, friend, daughter, son, woman, man—they are roles. This is fine. We can play any of those roles. We must just remember our essence and remember what is truly important—the connection with our soul, with the source, the pure energy, the divine spark inside us.

Do you see this book as a journey into the real essence?

Yes. To get back to the essence we need to start peeling away the layers. To peel the layers away, we need to get to know ourselves and who we really are. One stage after another, we must peel off the layers of gender, of ego, of what we have learned, of how we were educated, of what has been expected of us, and what we want to prove. These are things that aren't truly who we are; they aren't your true tune. They are what cover and conceal who we really are. They are costumes we wear. When we become aware of these costumes, we are able to take them off.

Be able to wear it, yet take it off at will. I loved the idea.

Wear it. That's fine. Just so long as you know it's a costume. On Halloween, when we dress up, we know we are wearing a costume. We don't believe it. We know who we are.

During the process of connecting with ourselves, we identify with the costume we wear less and less. We learn to recognize our own truth, our own essence. We become familiar with who we really are.

Exactly. It is only when people know who they really are—when they reach their essence, their precise individual sound—that harmony will exist in the world. Right now, there is chaos because there is no synchronicity. We are not synchronized with each other because we are not synchronized with ourselves.

What do you mean by being synchronized with ourselves?

Being synchronized with ourselves means to, first and foremost, understand who we really are. We must be able to separate our essence from the different costumes we wear and the roles we play. They are merely the instrument, the vehicle. Your essence is inside that vehicle, but you are the one who decides where to drive it, and what your vision is. In order to make this precise, we need first to understand the vehicle we are driving, our instrument, and the roles we have, even before we get to the essence, to the soul.

One of the first channeling messages I received was that the human body is the temple of the soul—so care for it. Familiarize yourself with it. Ask whether you feel comfortable inside your body.

Know yourself as a human being. Do you think negatively or positively? What are your feelings? What are your walls, your barriers? Know the things that you and I have spoken about here. When you understand what your essential will is, what your vision is, then you can start to fulfill it.

Shari's words matched the knowledge I had already received. The soul has a personality. It directs us to what is right (or not right) for us, based on our personality and our abilities. Sometimes, when we try to do something, an inner resistance appears in us.

It is important to stop to understand where this is coming from. It may come from the voice of the soul which is telling us what we want to do does not fit with our deeper, truer will. Our true will reflects who we really are.

Often, our inner need is to help others—to develop, to bring knowledge. That comes from our true, essential will. We all have unique desires, but we do not always listen to them. The essential will creates a sort of inner urge to do things; a sense of mission.

Was that what Shari meant when she talks about vision?

Our vision is what we want to fulfill in all the circles of life. It involves our health, our thoughts, our feelings, our actions, our families. What do we want to fulfill for the world? The vision touches all of life's circles.

But, if I get to know my essence, perhaps my will might change? I feel that the vision is very connected to the essence. If I feel great, then my vision can be great too, but if I feel small, I can't even bring myself to think about a great vision.

Because the soul is in the body, we usually do not see the soul's will. We keep dealing with the will of the body, the costumes, the ego—a new car, a bigger apartment, relationships, children, making a living, surviving. None of those things are about the true will of the soul.

So, how do we get to know the soul's will? Only if we peel away the layers will we reach that authentic soulful calling. I believe our vision comes from our soulful calling, but we often get confused, because many other components infiltrate into this vision—components that do not come from the pure soul.

That does not mean that the vision isn't good or worthy. For many years, I've had grand visions, like building the Medical Tower in Tel Aviv, or by establishing Matan— Your Way of Giving, to create a culture of giving and community involvement in the Israeli business sector.

I did many things that originated in these visions, but many years had to pass before I realized that the real question isn't what have I done, but, rather, where did the will to do these things come from?

It was then that I realized that I have done a lot of things and fulfilled many visions because I wanted to prove myself; to show everyone I could do it and prove that I am a good and caring person. Those visions came from a place of low ego. Had I known and understood that sooner, perhaps I would still have done the same things, but it would have come from being whole and connected to my soul. The energy would have been different.

The process I am undergoing in this book comes from a very tranquil and peaceful place. I don't feel the pressure of time, or the pressure of proving myself. I have had a lot of dreams and a lot of visions that were accompanied by many battles. I have done many amazing things. I introduced the concept of "financial freedom" to the bank I owned at the time, and the concept of "sustainability" to a real estate and infrastructure company that I owned. However, everything was accompanied by struggles—many, many struggles.

It is why it is so important to be precise with your vision; to know that it comes from the right place, from positive, pure energy. It can be a personal vision or a general one. What sort of life do I want? What sort of life would I like to see on the face of the Earth? In the universe? There are those whose will has more to do with their personal lives, while others have a wider range that has to do with their community, their environment, and the world.

Why is it important for us to have a vision?

When you fish, you throw the line as far as you can, and then pull it back. It is important that we have a vision of a better world, because, to fulfill it in the future, we need to dream it first; see it. The vision is important for us, for humanity. If every one of us had dreamed of a better world in the past, we would be living in it already.

So having vision means thinking of a situation that is better than the current one?

For me, having vision is something that is useful, but its usefulness isn't necessarily material, it is something of a higher value, deep and wide.

To change the world, I said smiling.

To change the world, to benefit the world, to bring the world to a better place. To return the world to the essence of God.

That is my vision too, I thought quietly. For a moment, I felt the gap between us once again. Shari has done things on a grand scale. I have not. And still, the need to turn the world into a better place, and for our lives to be more fulfilling and meaningful, literally burns in me.

I think that today there are many people who share the same dream, even if they are only able to do it on a smaller scale.

There's no such thing as a smaller scale. We need to understand how important and essential it is. While individuals empower the whole, many people question themselves, who am I to change the world? If there were more people to hold this dream in their consciousness, this vision of a better world, one that is purer, more moral, and friendly, then together we would be able to fulfill it. We need to sustain the dream.

We also need to know which energy brings the vision and its realization. For example, when you say we will fight for peace, we generate a fight-like energy, and that energy brings a battle. If you want peace, you need to lead the way to peace—promote peace. You say there are a lot of people who share the vision, but they embark on struggles.

I took a moment to consider what is taking place around us—all the struggles that surround us. Struggles for change. I, too, often feel that I am at war as I am trying to advance and develop my dream. It is a battle mainly within myself, with my own fears, doubts, and dilemmas. Even the will to advance is perceived as a sort of struggle. We use aggressive terms, such as "breaking through," and "fighting over." Those are the kinds of expression I use when I think about my business development, for example.

I have to admit, I've never considered it in quite that way. What could I say instead of "I would like to break through with my business?"

I'd like to grow; be empowered. I'd like to move forward.

But doesn't it have a completely different energy? I expressed my doubts in a question.

And it is exactly that completely different energy that will lead to the right fulfillment. The right energy.

But saying, "I am going to expand my business," is nothing like saying, "I am going to fight to expand my business."

Fighting is about survival. Survival engenders survival. We need to free ourselves from that circle and choose words related to growth, expansion, progress, and renewal. It is a different energy.

Take the term fighting against corruption. Why can't we encourage integrity, promote better values, and seek transparency? Some people think that struggle is what brings fulfillment of the vision, but it brings separation.

I allowed myself to be lost in thought for a moment, as I promised myself I would think more about the subject soon.

What Does "Observing" Mean For You?

Looking back, my experience is that I have gone through several incarnations in a single lifetime. Normally, the soul reincarnates, the body dies, and the soul leaves the body and elevates. It then enters another body and starts another incarnation.

I feel I have gone through many incarnations without dying and coming back—all of those incarnations being in this life. My childhood and teenage years were one incarnation. Each of my three marriage periods were incarnations. A fifth was a meaningful relationship I had—that was perhaps the most meaningful incarnation.

In this current incarnation I am alone, building my independence and my inner being, my self-appreciation and love, and my will for a much more intimate mission.

In my first incarnation, my childhood and my teens, I felt like I did not belong on this planet, as though I had arrived in the wrong world. I could not understand the separation, the being apart, the cruelty and suffering. I had to transcend all that; learn a lesson.

Each of my marriages was a different chapter in my life. In each, I lived in completely different worlds, in a different culture, with different food and a different vibe and lifestyle. Those periods taught me to realize my ability to jump between all the worlds. It taught me to recognize the feeling that I did not truly belong in any single place, resulting from the fact that I belonged to all places.

I learned to express myself, to bridge the gap between the manner and intensity with which I see and feel things—in images, in experiences, in sensations and feelings, and in my ability to express them in writing. It was a gap that had kept me stuck for many years. Today, in retrospect, I can see that my development has always taken place through expression, both between me and myself, and between myself and others—to communicate in a positive, constructive, and bridging way.

That is the main goal in all of my life's circles, but in my previous incarnations I simply did not have the words to convey all that. At that time, all I could see was my difficulty in expressing myself, but today I know this was my main goal.

I thought about myself and about all my students. One of the things that disrupts our lives the most is our fear of expressing ourselves. This goes far beyond expression. It is the ability to feel, to know, to understand what is going on with us and what is right for us. We are afraid of being criticized, afraid of not being loved, of being rejected and laughed at. And in our pain, we keep silent. We feel trapped.

I thought about myself. When I first realized I possessed channeling abilities, I was frightened. I did not want anyone to know about it. I was surrounded by rational people and thought they would despise me and my "craziness." As time passed, more and more of my friends became more familiar with my abilities and, much to my surprise, I received no disrespect. On the contrary, I was more appreciated by them. This empowered me and gave me the courage to continue and express my inner world.

Shari has also gone through a significant process of self development. She has progressed from a place of great difficulty in expressing herself to a point where she is able to express herself in the way she wants.

How did you reach this situation where you are able to bridge that gap and are able to express yourself?

Using a lot of methods, many paths, books, facilitators, and workshops, I have continuously looked for ways of expressing myself better, of bringing myself into any situation and communication in more complete ways.

So, expressing yourself is about daring to bring out who you really are, I thought aloud.

Yes. I think your expression reflects the place you are at in any particular moment. My expression has gradually improved as my inner being has improved. It became tranquil, more powerful, and more precise. Sometimes I still feel the gaps, because my vision is so wide and my experience and sensations are so powerful that expressing them in words diminishes and narrows them.

What else have you learned in your incarnations?

I've also learned how to observe. I am a constant observer. Every moment, every hour. I observe even in my sleep. I observe all the time.

Are you observing now?

Of course. Always. Even as we speak I am observing my own thoughts, my feelings, my sensations, my physical state, my emotional experience, the interaction between you and me, and more. It is a skill.

In the past, I had to learn to decipher what I saw. What sort of thoughts I'm thinking, what sort of feelings I'm experiencing, why I'm feeling what I'm feeling, what the person in front of me is projecting, is there a gap, or not. But today, it all happens simultaneously. Observation is happening at every given moment.

And do you learn about yourself through this observing? Does it help you to understand what is going on with you? To understand why you behave in the way you do? What does this constant observing allow you?

I think that my observation is very different from that of another person, because we are all built differently. We each need to find our own individual way of observing. But observation, in itself, helps us to understand who we really are.

Sometimes, when a person observes as much as I do, they realize there is no separation. My feelings are connected to all my layers, inside and out.

There is the personal layer—what happened to me in the moments before you arrived here, how well I slept during the night, how I got up, and even what I dreamed. Then there is the general layer. I am aware that I feel many things that aren't mine at all, that I am able to feel the collective energy. All these layers comprise who I am right now, at this very second, and it can change in a moment.

You have a very gentle and enabling way of guiding people. You talk about things as a suggestion, not as a necessity, which is what makes it so powerful. It comes from a very intimate place.

That's right. Every incarnation had its own significance, and my current incarnation is one of intimacy. Intimacy with myself, intimacy with my path and my mission, intimacy with my will to move on to the next stage of my life. I think that through this intimacy something has opened up in me; something enabling, which is what I want.

Going through so many incarnations in one life must have been challenging at times. What has been the source of your strength?

I know that a lot of people may think, oh, it's because she's rich, but that doesn't have anything to do with it. It has to do with which reality you want to create. I'm not talking about getting rich. I'm talking about the freedom to be the person you wish to be, who you really are. It is about what your essence is, about how you express your essence. Everything is open.

What is Your Mission?

Since our last meeting I have been thinking a lot about the significant process that Shari and I have gone through, both together and separately. More and more, I was able to see the similarities between us, although the differences were still there. Those differences were not just about our financial situation, but had also to do with our individual life experiences, which have simply been different.

Nevertheless, there are many similarities—a real connection. We share similar attitudes to life as well as a belief in goodness and, mainly, our desire to bring good into the world, each of us in our own way.

I thought about the inner urge that propels the two of us, and many others, to do what we need to do—even when the way becomes hard and uncertain, even when the path becomes unknown. We call this the inner voice the voice of the soul, or, simply, our mission.

When did you start feeling that you had a mission?

Always. I've always felt I have a mission from my soul. That I have come here for a reason, that I am supposed to help humanity to change. Even in my younger years,

I always took each difficulty and turned it into a learning experience.

What do you mean?

If I had a certain difficulty—and there were many . . . .

Shari was silent for a moment and then smiled.

I am going over some of the writings I've collected throughout my life. I found diaries that I wrote when I was nine, ten, thirteen—when I was between worlds, between Israel and America. It amazes me to read them now, across the space of time.

I wrote about financial difficulties at home during my childhood, about wanting certain things that we could not afford, about difficulties with the differences in cultures, difficulties with relationships in the family and with friends, with romantic relationships, and with personal development.

Then there was the sudden shift from having little money to becoming rich, which happened when I was almost thirty. I wrote about difficulties in philanthropic endeavors and in business and financial management. Great wealth may sound impressive, but managing it is no small feat. There were difficulties with communication or the assimilation of values and a lot more. I observed each of these things as something that had been given to me by God, by the universe, so I could learn firsthand, so I could help other people to learn and make use of it.

I looked at Shari with a smile on my lips. You've always felt you were experiencing these things firsthand, for the general good?

Yes, but it was more than merely experiencing things for myself. Other things go through me as well. I feel I somehow absorb public difficulty and transform it into more positive energy, transform it into light, and spread it. That is what keeps me going, the fact that I am here for this mission.

A mission comes at all dimensions and circles. Your mission with yourself, with your family, with those surrounding you. In fact, the mission gradually grows to cover many dimensions and many, many circles, and you mustn't neglect any of these. We are not detached. Everything is connected to everything, and your mission too, involves all circles and dimension.

I admired Shari's words and they got me thinking. I thought about how each of us has a different mission. Many times, we tend to use the term mission only for grander, world-changing things, but, in my eyes a mission is the inner feeling of a person; an urge to act in a certain way.

When we refer only to the grander things as a mission, we cancel out, or reduce, the great things we do in the day-to-day. Shari has done, and is still doing, wonderful things on a grand scale. This is definitely impressive, but it does not take anything away from the value of the smaller things many of us do.

Suddenly, I had the insight that it is when we look at those who do things on a grander scale with admiration and wonder, that we reduce the smaller things that we do on a daily basis. It is so important for us not to judge things. Every undertaking has its place, and sometimes a small thing may actually be very significant.

For a moment, I felt I was doing it again, comparing my actions with Shari's, but this time I stopped. There was no point in making such comparisons. The world needs every endeavor that can advance it, large or small, and every single person who contributes is significant. I felt a great pride in being numbered among the people who persist in searching for a way; the people who go on wanting to help and advance the world.

I felt that we are all blessed, regardless of the scope of our endeavors.

Is There An End?

Working together has created intimacy between us. We have spoken about things on a deeper, more profound level that we probably would never have reached without this process of joint writing.

When we started writing this book, I felt Shari's side as confronting my own. The gap between us made it difficult for me to see her objectively. Gradually, without really noticing, my biased views about Shari melted away, one by one. I was able to start seeing things from her viewpoint and, many times, I felt that being "Shari Arison" is not easy. Her status and endeavors came with a price.

Once again, I thought about those who find it easy to suspect Shari because of her status, people who would cast doubt on her words. In the past few years, Shari and I have become much closer. I no longer saw the icon in her, but the person.

When we started writing this book, I felt small next to Shari. It wasn't a logical feeling, and was certainly not there because Shari had made me feel that way, not at all. She has been nothing short of charming to me from day one. I was the one who held on to a gap between us.

Even though I did not mean to, I know I was looking at Shari with some kind of doubt. Yes, it has taken me some time to trust her, and I assume it has taken Shari some time to trust me. In the process of writing, I came to feel more and more significant.

Rereading this book, I can actually feel in its pages the long process I have gone through. How our many conversations—the many things we have shared, our consultations—have made me feel that I, too, have much to give; both to Shari and to others. To a certain extent, this book has connected me with who I truly am, and for that, I am very happy.

Toward the end of our work on the book, I asked Shari, and how should we end this book? Shari looked at me and smiled.

We simply finish the writing, but the process never ends.

What do you mean?

The process of getting to know ourselves never ends. Every time we look at things, observe them, we will discover new layers. That is the beauty of this process.

It's like you said in the opening pages, this is a book of growth and personal development that readers should come back to again and again.
Shari smiled.

Exactly so.

What is Your Sense of Time?

I have been rereading this book as it comes closer to publication, and I find it funny to read over and over about how we had sat together in my office.

A year has passed since—a year that has been dominated by the coronavirus pandemic. So much has changed—for each of us individually, and for the whole world.

It has been a year of ups and down, of inner pain, and pain generated by everything that has been happening around us. There has been an overwhelming sense of fear, anger, and frustration, and much time spent in solitude, and with my family. It has been a time for reflection, a time for an advanced evolution in which all wrongs come to the surface and are cleansed to make room for a new world.

During the past few months, I have found myself diving deep into my soul, into my body, releasing a deep pain that is accompanied by sadness and endless anger. Is it mine? Is it the surroundings? Both are one and the same to me.

It isn't a simple process, but it is one that is bringing me to a deepening and further understanding of who I really am. We keep changing shape all the time, transforming, discovering something new about ourselves, another aspect, one more angle. The process of discovery is endless. I wish for you, our reader, that you will be able to discover yourself and bring the most enlightened version of yourself to the world.

I feel as if time has accelerated and yet simultaneously stopped. As if everything I have done up to now, this book and all the messages contained in it, have come at just the right time for this moment in 2022. It is a time in which we—both as individuals and as humanity—can make a choice. To choose the new, the light, to choose the good. What will you choose?